Ladies First

Ladies First

Titanic's Reckoning with Wealth and Worth

By Alina Rush

Unbound Press

Ladies First: Titanic's Reckoning with Wealth and Worth

Fault Lines: Book 2

Alina Rush

ISBN Paperback ISBN: 978-1-971207-25-4

ISBN Hardcover ISBN: 978-1-971207-26-1

The Fault Lines Series

The Fault Lines series examines moments when progress, confidence, and modern systems collide—and fail. These books focus not on spectacle or hindsight, but on the underlying fractures that disasters expose: labor rendered invisible, class shaping survival, technology trusted beyond its limits, and institutions slow to confront their own assumptions.

Beginning with the Titanic trilogy and extending to crises such as the economic disparities of the Great Depression, the series traces how economic, social, and technological fault lines run beneath seemingly stable worlds. Each volume grounds its narrative in verifiable history while centering the experiences of ordinary people caught inside extraordinary events—workers, immigrants, families, and communities whose lives bore the actual cost of collapse.

Fault Lines is not a history of accidents. It is a study of systems under stress, of warnings ignored, and of the human consequences that follow when risk is unevenly distributed. These are stories about how societies break—and what those breaks reveal long after the headlines fade.

Table of Contents

Dedication

For the women and children. For the engineers who stayed.
For the stewards and stewardesses who knocked on every
door they could reach. For the ones the record kept, and the
ones it didn't.

Forever in our hearts.

Introduction

Women and Children First

The phrase "Women and Children First" did not originate with the Titanic, but it was on that ship that the rule became a myth. In the decades since the disaster, it has been repeated as evidence of Edwardian chivalry—proof that, in extremes, society protected its most vulnerable. The reality was more complicated, more uneven, and more revealing.

On the night of April 14, 1912, the instruction to prioritize women and children was neither universal nor consistently enforced. It was filtered through class, geography, authority, and timing. Where a woman stood on the ship—physically and socially—often mattered as much as her gender. The rule did not operate in a vacuum. It operated on a vessel already divided by design.

Titanic was not one ship but several stacked vertically. First-class women were closest to the boat deck, spoke the language of the crew, and were accustomed to deference. Second and third-class women slept deep below, navigated unfamiliar corridors, and often traveled alone or with children in tow. Between them were the ship's working women—stewardesses—tasked with maintaining order, comfort, and calm, even as the situation deteriorated.

The rule women and children first was never written into maritime law. It was custom, not statute. Custom depends on who enforces it, who obeys it, and who is able to benefit from it. On Titanic, enforcement varied by officer. Obedience varied by passenger. Access varied by class.

For some women, the instruction functioned as intended. They were awakened early, guided to the deck, and placed into lifeboats with relative speed. For others, the rule arrived too late, or not at all. Some never heard it, and others physically could not reach the lifeboats. Some faced constraints because of language barriers, locked passageways, or the simple arithmetic of distance and time.

The survival statistics tell only part of the story. Women survived at higher rates than men overall, but that headline obscures sharp internal divisions. First-class women survived at extraordinary rates. Third-class women did not. Children's survival depended almost entirely on class and age, as we will see from the story of Rhoda Abbott. Gender alone did not save lives; proximity, privilege, and help did.

The phrase also obscures the cost borne by women whose labor made evacuation possible. Stewardesses guided passengers, translated instructions, distributed lifejackets, and maintained order in the corridors. Many delayed their own escape or never attempted it. Their adherence to duty—shaped by employment, gender expectations, and obedience—became another invisible factor in who lived and who did not.

Women and children first was not a promise. It was a principle unevenly applied on a divided ship. Understanding what it actually meant—who benefited from it, who enforced it, and who paid for it—reveals far more about the Titanic than the myth ever has.

This is not a story of chivalry fulfilled. It is a reckoning with how gender and class interacted under pressure, and how those interactions shaped the outcomes of one of the most scrutinized disasters in modern history.

Part I — A Society Under Steam

Chapter 1 — A Ship of the Gilded Age

What we call the Gilded Age is but the glittering surface of a deeper struggle.

— Mark Twain

The Turkish Baths, April 14, 1912

THE TURKISH BATHS WERE tucked within the heart of the ship, below the promenade and away from the Atlantic wind, where heat could be sustained, and illusion perfected. The Edwardian fascination with the "Oriental" bath—heat, tile, ritual purification—had traveled from London clubs to Atlantic liners, and White Star understood that first-class women expected more than cabins and courses. They expected experience. The baths were part of that promise, and maintaining them required precision.

To step inside was to forget the ocean. Tile replaced timber, and vibrant mosaic floors gleamed under electric light. Geometric designs of an Eastern motif patterned the walls in turquoise and cream. Marble basins curved outward like open palms, and brass fixtures shone against the warmth. Neatly stacked white, thick towels waited to be unfurled by women of privilege.

Steam permeated the air. Not heavy or oppressive but controlled. Designed. A gentle hum from the ship's hidden machinery filled the room, muffled by tile and plaster. The baths were insulated from motion. Here, Titanic did not feel like steel and rivets. She felt like a hotel in Cairo or a private club in London. Heat, tile, and order: a sanctuary within steel.

Recreation of Turkish Bath, Titanic

First-class women entered wrapped in robes, speaking in low voices about Paris, about Fifth Avenue, and about the bracing air on deck. The bath softened them. Heat loosened conversation. Slippers slid against tile. Jewelry was removed and placed carefully aside. Gloves folded, and hair loosened from pins. The ritual was deliberate. Light reflected off the marble, and outside, the April air in the Atlantic Ocean remained sharp and cold.

A warm room first, to allow the body to adjust. Then hotter air, encouraging perspiration. Cooling rooms afterward, with chairs arranged for rest beneath electric sconces. Some women lingered to read. The Atlantic felt far away.

The baths were not merely a service, but a statement: to bathe at sea was to experience civilization on the water; that refinement need not yield to salt and wind. It meant the Atlantic could be crossed without surrendering comfort.

Admission required a first-class ticket, where class was softened but not erased. The attendants kept the system intact. Maude Slocombe was among them, checking the temperature of the steam chamber and ensuring the basins were properly filled and drained. She arranged combs and brushes where they would be easy to find. She refreshed the towels and ensured the baths were spotless. Maude understood that luxury is maintained through invisibility. The room must feel effortless, as if the towels were folding themselves. Maude's presence was part of the illusion: calm, competent, and discreet.

It is difficult to imagine a greater contrast: below decks, immigrant mothers wrapped infants against the draft; above, women reclined in warmth, insulated from the Atlantic's bite. And on the night of April 14, when the tremor moved through steel and tile alike, steam shivered almost imperceptibly before settling again. At first, it felt like nothing more than an interruption—a minor correction in motion.

The illusion held for a few minutes longer.

Heat lingered, towels remained folded, but outside breath was visible, the stars bright and indifferent. The boat deck was alive now with motion that did not resemble leisure, and the ocean was pressing against the hull below. Maude did what she had been hired to do, moving women toward safety. She spoke in a steady tone and trusted the structure above her. Luxury had been her department. Now survival was.

And the line between them was thinner than tile.

<hr>

Titanic's story began in the spring of 1909, on the gray edge of Belfast Lough, where men in flat caps and heavy boots walked beneath a wall of steel. Above them, the ribs of a new ship—Yard Number 401—rose higher than any building in the city. She was not yet called Titanic. She was an idea first: an answer to rival shipping lines, a promise of crossing the sea in unmatched comfort and safety. Their boots struck timber planks slick with rain.

At the turn of the century, the Atlantic had become a corridor of competition, as empires traded people and goods across the North Atlantic. Cunard boasted speed, while other lines promised glamour, famous passengers, and record-breaking passages.

The White Star Line responded with a different promise: not just the fastest crossing, but the most comfortable and prestigious way to reach America. From this promise came a trio of great liners, the Olympic-class ships—Olympic, Titanic, and a planned third sister, later named Britannic— intended to command the Atlantic in 1911, 1912, and 1913. They would not race the ocean; they would dominate it.

In Belfast, the shipyard reshaped itself to meet that ambition. Gantries climbed higher than church spires. On March 31, 1909, workers laid the keel, and from that line of steel, the skeleton climbed.

Riveters hammered red-hot bolts into place, sparks falling like brief, furious stars. Workers hoisted and fixed steel plates, and the hull thickened day by day against wind and tide. For more than two years, the work did not stop. Nearby sheds turned out fittings for cabins that would rival grand hotels on land. White Star's goal was clear: a ship large enough to carry wealthy travelers in luxury and, at the same time, to move thousands of emigrants in third-class and hundreds of crew members across the ocean in a steady, profitable stream. Speed mattered, but prestige mattered more.

Titanic was designed to carry about 2,435 passengers and around 900 crew, a small floating city divided by class and function, yet sharing the same steel hull and the same cold ocean. Her designers built in fifteen watertight bulkheads and doors that could be closed from the bridge, a system widely praised at the time and often cited as a reason she was described in newspapers and advertisements as practically "unsinkable."

The Launch

At 6 am on Tuesday, 2 April 1912, as people along the lough watched her slide into the water, a single firework exploded against a turquoise sky to announce the moment. Women in hats stood beside factory workers, and people lifted children onto their shoulders. The ship—still hollow and unfinished—moved down greased slipways and entered the gray sea to the sound of whistles and cheers.

She was named Titanic, and she was already famous, already a symbol of what modern steel and steam could achieve.

Even unfinished, she was the largest moving object ever made by human hands. Inside her hull, for nearly a year more, carpenters, electricians, upholsterers, and decorators turned steel into rooms. Carpenters carved English oak into panels that replicated those in the Palace of Versailles. Staircases rose beneath glass domes. Carpets were chosen with debate and patience. Below, emigrants who had never seen electric light in their own homes would find cabins fitted with iron bunks and enamel washstands.

The ship was becoming layered, not only by deck but also by expectation.

Titanic departing Belfast for sea trials on 2 April 1912. Public Domain.

Luxury and Distance

Ten decks rose above the Atlantic, each one narrowing the field of experience. From the outside, the ship appeared unified—a sweep of steel and funnels, a society under steam. Inside, it divided itself.

First Class

First class was theater. Passengers entered through wide gangways into corridors trimmed in polished wood and brass. Electric light—still a marvel to many travelers— glowed steadily from chandeliers and wall sconces.

Rooms were not uniform; they were themed. First-class suites featured walls with motifs inspired by Jacobean halls, as if European heritage could be contained within steel. English oak paneling was carved in relief; drawing rooms reflected Louis XVI style; French gilt and carved balustrades decorated the spaces; and the grand staircase rose beneath a glass dome. Versailles had been miniaturized and encased in steel. Designers recreated aristocratic interiors within the hull of a steamship, compressing centuries of taste into a single voyage. Here, history floated. Telephones, a marvel of their time, were even installed.

We think of Titanic in black and white, but in reality, it was saturated with color. Velvet. Polished wood. Gilt trim catching the electric light. Forest green carpets lay against ornate wallpaper designs in orange and red. The upholstery was rich, burnished gold. Carpet selection alone occupied the designers for two hours. The question of how many lifeboats were needed would be asked and answered in 15 minutes. After all, it was designed to reassure the wealthy, not to anticipate failure.

First Class Bedroom on Titanic

The famous grand staircase rose beneath a glass dome, its balustrades crafted with precision. There were four dining rooms, à la carte restaurants and a Parisian café. There were smoking rooms, sitting rooms, and writing rooms. There was the Turkish bath, a squash court, and a gymnasium with mechanical horses and rowing devices allowing for exercise at sea. The message was clear: civilization need not surrender to the ocean.

Second Class

Second class did not glitter, but it did not apologize either. The corridors were painted in light tones that softened sconces' electric glow. There was no carved oak or gilt, just polished wood trim and clean lines. Cabins were compact but private. Iron bedsteads fixed to the wall and crisp white bedding stretched tight. Hooks for coats. A narrow wardrobe. A mirror that did not flatter, but did not distort.

The Second-Class Dining Saloon lay on the Saloon Deck, broad and orderly, capable of seating hundreds at long, neatly arranged tables. White tablecloths under proper china, and silver polished to a quiet shine. No orchestra swelled here, no carved ceiling overhead—but the service was steady and correct. Meals arrived in courses. Soup steamed in porcelain bowls, and bread was passed hand-to-hand.

Second-Class Dining on Titanic

This room hosted a different kind of conversation. Not about estates and inheritances, but about positions secured or waiting. A clerkship beginning in Chicago. Letters received, wages expected, or a school term in Boston. A husband establishing himself in Seattle, or a new position in a Vermont household. Second class was full of people mid-trajectory.

There was a library where mahogany chairs stood beneath shelves of books. Writing desks faced windows where the Atlantic stretched in steel-blue calm. Women wrote letters by electric light—reassurances sent ahead, descriptions of the ship's steadiness, remarks about the chilly April air on deck. Men withdrew to the Smoking Room, its walls paneled in dark wood, its air thick with talk and tobacco.

On clear afternoons, passengers walked the open deck assigned to them, leaning into the wind that smelled of salt and coal smoke. The railings were polished brass, deck planks clean and pale beneath sensible shoes. Children darted between deckchairs. Mothers called them back.

Second class occupied a middle altitude on the ship— close enough to glimpse first-class elegance if one knew where to look, far enough above steerage to avoid its density. The staircases were narrower, but they were navigable and direct. Movement upward required less negotiation. This mattered, though no one yet knew it would.

For second-class passengers, the voyage felt modern, measured, and attainable. There was no spectacle here. They had not purchased extravagance. They had purchased passage with dignity. And for four days, the ship delivered exactly what had been promised.

Third Class

Below, assurance thinned. Third class would carry the future of the Atlantic migration: Irish girls bound for domestic service, Scandinavian laborers, Jewish mothers

traveling alone with infants, and boys just tall enough to
call themselves nearly men.

Advertisement for Third Class, Titanic

The accommodations were not squalor, but containment.
Third-class cabins were small and stacked deep within the
hull. They were enclosed, not open berths, arranged in
compartments toward the lower decks where they felt the
hum of electrical systems below. Bedding was provided,
and meals were served in common dining rooms rather
than requiring passengers to cook their own provisions.
Privacy was limited, and families were grouped by gender
and status according to regulation. Corridors were
narrower, but for many immigrants, this was progress.

Earlier generations had crossed in open berths with little
sanitation and less privacy. Titanic offered dignity. Families
could close a door. The décor did not mimic Versailles, but
utility. There was a small washbasin fitted with running

water, an indulgence for many travelers who had known only shared pumps ashore.

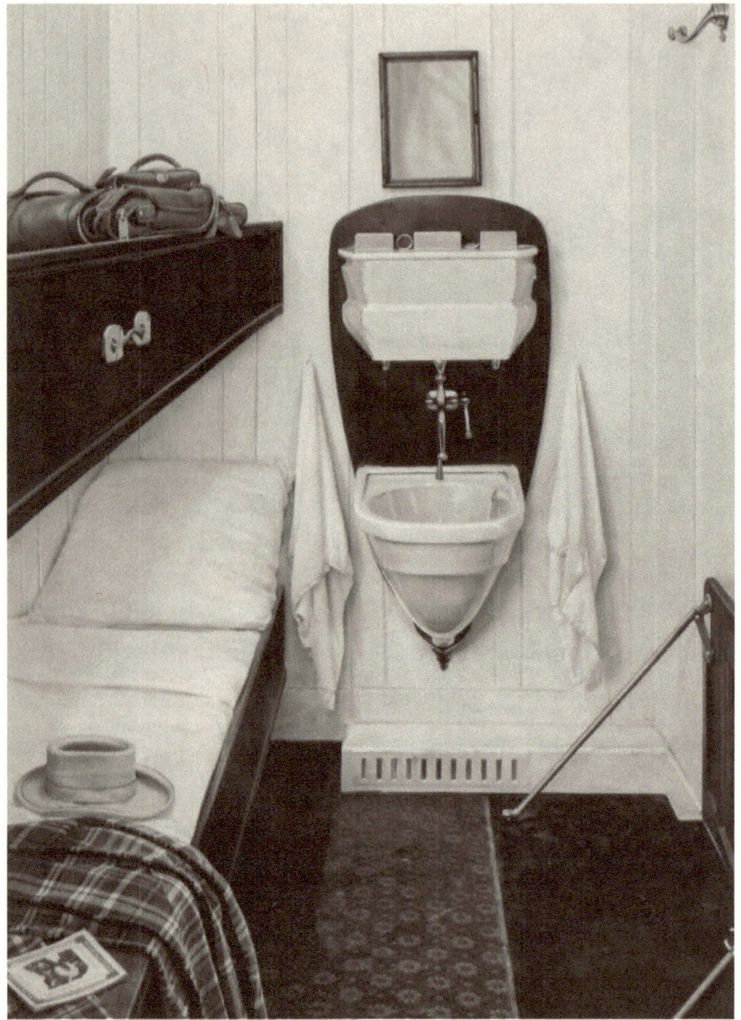

Third Class Accommodations

Yet even here, color existed. Light came from electric fixtures, yes—but without chandeliers or gilt. Iron bunks with green-and-white bedding replaced carved bedsteads.

The ship felt modern and hopeful. The modern age had reached even here.

The physical space between a third-class cabin and the boat deck was measured in stairways, turns, and time. This distance mattered. The difference between a first-class woman's promenade and a steerage mother's bunk was not merely aesthetic. It was logistical.

Titanic recreation of Stairwell

Women at Sea in 1912

Ocean travel had become faster, safer, and more common by the early twentieth century, but it remained structured by class and by ideas about propriety. Steamships stitched continents together with iron certainty, carrying bankers, their brides, governesses, and girls with trunks tied with twine. By 1912, women at sea were no longer novel, but their presence was still constrained—legally, socially, and economically. The ticket a woman carried did not erase societal expectations.

Maritime culture remained rigidly male, hierarchical, and governed by assumptions about female dependence. Titanic did not challenge those assumptions; it accommodated them.

Legally, women in 1912 occupied a narrow space. Married women's identities were largely subsumed under their husbands'. Property rights varied by country. Custody of children, access to wages, and freedom of movement were all shaped by marital status. A woman traveling alone was not assumed to be independent by default; she was often treated as temporary, vulnerable, or suspect.

For women, crossing the Atlantic was rarely casual. It was undertaken because something on the other side demanded it. It meant migration, employment, marriage, or family obligation. Middle- and upper-class women traveled with chaperones, servants, or husbands. Working-class women often traveled alone or with children, shouldering the burden of resettlement. These distinctions mattered long before the iceberg appeared.

Economic Necessity vs. Choice

For a small minority of women, the voyage was elective: a return from holiday, an extended tour, a fashionable crossing on the newest liner afloat. These were the passengers of First Class who inhabited cabins trimmed in carved wood and wrote letters describing the elegance of the staircase. They promenaded under supervision and dined according to ritual. Their presence at sea was an extension of their refinement onshore; the crossing framed as an experience.

Even among the wealthy, economic structures exerted influence. Marriage alliances, inheritance strategies, and social positioning traveled alongside trunks of silk. A young bride crossing the Atlantic was not merely relocating; she was cementing an arrangement with financial implications far beyond romance.

For many others, the journey was a calculation.

Second class was full of people between stories, and women occupied the middle ground. Schoolteachers returning from positions abroad, widows resettling with family, and skilled workers moving toward new employment. Irish and Scandinavian women traveled to domestic service positions arranged in advance. Eastern European women boarded understanding that factory or garment work awaited them. Some traveled to marry men they had not seen in years, or, in some cases, had never met. Their movement was part of a broader economic choreography of families diversifying risk across oceans. They were meant to be orderly, self-regulating, and grateful.

A single mother boarding a steamship did not do so lightly. The fare might represent years of savings. The decision might follow crop failure, factory closure, or the quiet arithmetic of widowhood. Economic necessity did not announce itself dramatically; it pressed steadily until departure felt inevitable.

Third-class women traveled in numbers that startled the imagination. They boarded with infants bundled in shawls, with siblings in tow, and with letters of introduction folded carefully into bodices. Their voyage was often the hinge of a family's survival. The passage purchased with pooled wages and mortgaged land. Many had never seen the ocean before stepping onto it.

The ocean compressed these motives into shared space. On deck, women from radically different circumstances inhaled the same salt air. They shared corridors, though not quarters. They shared the rhythm of engines below, though not the view from the promenade. What they did not share equally was proximity to information, to authority, and to the physical exits that would matter later.

Travel Norms

Travel norms were both explicit and implicit. Women were expected to remain within assigned spaces, obey posted instructions, and defer to crew, to husbands, to the invisible machinery of order that kept the ship running on schedule. Deference was not weakness; it was the price of moving through a system built by men. Rules were not suggestions; they were survival tools. To obey instructions was to remain in good standing—with husbands, captains, and with governments waiting on distant shores. A woman who followed instructions was "respectable." A woman who resisted could be labeled difficult or untrustworthy.

Even the ship's architecture rehearsed these lessons. Beyond class, spaces were organized according to gendered perceptions of protection and the exercise of control. Cabins, lounges, and promenades for women were designed with the purpose of maintaining order, supervision, and segregation. Doors marked by class, stairways reserved, and gates were installed not for cruelty but for control. Separation was policy. A woman quickly learned where she was meant to stand. Third-class women were often far from exits and crew traffic.

Third Class women

For immigrant women, the journey carried additional risks. Many were young, unmarried, and traveling for work. Language barriers were common. Arrival in the United States did not guarantee entry; it required inspection, health clearance, and, in some cases, proof of moral character. A woman traveling alone could be questioned more intensively than a man. Was she joining a husband? Did she have an address? Was she "likely to become a public charge"? The phrase carried a financial judgment disguised as administrative neutrality.

These evaluations shaped behavior even before the voyage began. Documentation was carefully guarded.

Letters from sponsors were folded and refolded. Women understood that arrival was not guaranteed simply because passage had been paid.

The Education of Obedience

By the time a woman stepped aboard a great liner in 1912, she had been trained—by family, church, employer, and law—to value order. Obedience was not passive; it was strategic. It preserved reputation, protected children, and facilitated entry into systems. And those systems rewarded compliance. The woman who followed instructions found meals waiting. The woman who deferred to stewards found doors opened. The woman who trusted official instruction was reassured that all was well.

Such habits did not dissolve in crisis. They hardened.

The ship was therefore not a neutral passage. It was a testing ground. Women existed in suspension—between one system and another, between one name and possibly a new one. Marriage could transform status overnight, and widowhood could erase it. Women were continuously evaluated—by the crew, by immigration authorities, and by fellow passengers—on their behavior, appearance, and compliance.

Information as a Privilege

Titanic also did not distribute information evenly. In first class, communication moved through a web of staff and proximity. Passengers overheard things. Stewards relayed messages, and officers were diligent and visible. The ship's official and unofficial information traveled faster because the people who mattered most to the company were concentrated in one area and served by the greatest number of staff.

In steerage, information could arrive late, in fragments, or not at all. Part of this was structural: fewer staff, more passengers, and less direct access to officers. Part of it was linguistic: steerage was multilingual, which slowed everything because every instruction became a two-step process when translation was needed.

This is where interpreters and bilingual passengers became critical. A single person who understood English could turn noise into meaning and panic into direction. Without interpreters—formal or informal—steerage passengers were left to interpret tone, gesture, and rumor.

These expectations and legal constraints shaped behavior during crises and reflected how women understood authority. Trust in male authority was not irrational; it had been rewarded all along. Deference had kept women safe, fed, and housed during the voyage. Obedience was a survival strategy in ordinary circumstances. On Titanic, it became a liability for some and a lifeline for others.

It is tempting to read the disaster backward and assume women should have acted differently—fought harder, moved faster, or disobeyed sooner. That judgment overlooks the world they inhabited. In 1912, women were taught that safety came from order, and order from compliance. The outcomes were not simply the result of panic or heroism in the last hours. They were the culmination of expectations built into the voyage itself— expectations about who belonged where, who gave orders, and who was meant to wait. The iceberg did not create those rules. It exposed them.

———————————❖———————————

Working Women: Stewardesses and Shipboard Labor

Titanic was built to carry roughly 2,400 passengers and nearly 900 crew—a small city at sea. Of these crewmembers, there were working women, a category entirely different from that of passengers or officers. If first-class women moved through velvet and light, and third-class women through narrow corridors and iron gates, stewardesses moved between worlds.

Stewardesses lived between classes, moved through restricted spaces, and were expected to embody calm authority without exercising actual power. They would walk corridors with keys at their waists, and bath attendants would keep the steam rooms immaculate. Matrons were tasked with supervising female steerage passengers; to manage women and children—to soothe, guide, and quietly discipline—while remaining subordinate to male command. They would not glide down the grand staircase as guests. They would memorize it as terrain.

Female labor at sea was framed as an extension of domestic duty. Stewardesses cleaned cabins, assisted mothers, distributed linens, and enforced decorum. They were trained to reassure, not to question.

They slept in small crew quarters, rose before most passengers stirred, and worked until the ship quieted at night. Their uniforms signaled authority, but it was a borrowed kind of power and limitation at once. Dark fabric, a crisp apron, and sensible shoes. It provided trustworthiness, but not command. She was to manage comfort without control and enforce order without writing the rules. A stewardess could instruct a passenger to fasten a lifejacket, but she could not contradict an officer. She could soothe a frightened child, but she could not alter the route of the ship.

Southampton group photo of Titanic stewardesses, taken April 10, 1912. Left-to-right in standard archival references are: Katherine Elizabeth Smith, Lucy Violet Snape, Mary Jane "May" Sloan, Annie Robinson, Sarah Agnes Staples, Elizabeth Lavington, Violet Constance Jessop, Maude Louise Slocombe, Emily Margaret Borie, Unknown, Mary Ann "Mollie" Wilson, Elizabeth Mary Leather. Public Domain.

The stewardess stood close enough to privilege to see it clearly. She handled silk gloves and fur wraps, moving through carved staircases and carpeted corridors. She observed how wealth insulated discomfort. But proximity did not grant her entry. She could assist a first-class woman to a lifeboat; she could not insist on her own place beside

her. On a great liner in 1912, stewardesses were essential
and invisible at once.

Becoming a Stewardess

A stewardess did not wander onto a great liner by accident.
She arrived by reference.

In 1912, a woman seeking work at sea presented herself
not at the dock, as was typical for men, but at an office
across from a polished desk and the quiet scrutiny of a
clerk representing the White Star Line. She brought letters,
folded carefully in envelopes: testimonials from prior
employers, character attestations, and evidence that she
could be trusted with keys, property, and other people's
privacy.

Respectability was currency. Most stewardesses had
previous experience in domestic service, hotel
housekeeping, or hospital wards. They understood how to
move quietly through someone else's space. They knew the
choreography of care: how to make a bed so that no
wrinkle suggested haste, how to anticipate a request before
it was spoken, and how to absorb complaints without
escalating them. The company valued steadiness more than
glamour.

Training was less formal but rigorous in its expectations.
Learn the layout of the ship, memorize the decks, and know
which staircases led where. Understand the difference
between reassurance and panic. Never appear uncertain.
The Atlantic was unpredictable; the crew could not be.

Employment at sea also carried risks. Voyages were
long, seasickness was common, and hours were relentless.

Yet the wages, modest as they were, offered something rare for women: independence. A stewardess earned money without marrying for it. She saw cities beyond her birthplace. She handled currencies and languages, and she moved in proximity to wealth without possessing it.

Duties

A stewardess's work was often described as domestic at sea, but that phrase understates the scale and complexity of the role. She made beds, yes, and straightened cabins, but she also distributed blankets on deck, assisted elderly passengers, located lost luggage, and soothed anxious children. She knew which families required hot water at dawn and which ladies preferred tea before dressing.

She also functioned as translator, mediator, and quiet disciplinarian. Many stewardesses spoke multiple languages or could at least navigate the broken exchanges of migration. They helped interpret instructions for passengers who did not fully understand English, directed women to proper spaces, and maintained separation—by class, by decorum, and by expectation.

A stewardess was trained to trust orders because her livelihood depended on doing so. Questioning command was not merely insubordination; it was unthinkable within the culture of maritime hierarchy.

The work required stamina. Days were long, and the Atlantic was indifferent to fatigue. A stewardess was on call for seasickness, for spilled broth, for domestic disputes carried across water. She was expected to be calm, tidy, and firm without aggression. That expectation did not dissolve when the ship struck ice. The instinct formed by months or years of service would rise intact. When alarms sounded and passengers hesitated, stewardesses were among the first to move through corridors. Knock on doors, distribute jackets, and repeat instructions. Keep order. They told women to dress warmly. They told them to go to the lifeboats – or to wait. They told them it was precaution, not peril.

These women in uniform repeated instructions in steady voices, absorbing fear so others might remain calm. Their training had prepared them for panic in small doses—a frightened child, a passenger who fainted—but not for catastrophe. Yet the script remained the same: reassure, guide, maintain order.

When the phrase "women and children first" was invoked, it did not automatically dissolve this hierarchy. A stewardess was a woman, yes—but she was also crew. Her place in the evacuation depended not solely on gender but on classification. Was she a passenger or an employee? Protected or responsible?

The answer was not always clear.

Some stewardesses secured seats in lifeboats. Others did not. Several remained at their posts longer than was wise. Whether from loyalty, confusion, or obedience to instruction, they continued working after many passengers had begun to calculate escape.

Duty can be a tether.

When historians later counted survivors, stewardesses appeared in the column marked "women," but their experience cannot be reduced to that category alone. They were workers first, women second, in the company's logic, and both at once in the chaos of evacuation.

Chapter 2 — Boarding

◆◆

The sea has never been friendly to man. At most it has been the accomplice of human restlessness.

— Joseph Conrad, The Mirror of the Sea (1906)

FROM THE DOCK IN Southampton, she rose in steel and confidence, ten decks layered against the gray Atlantic sky. Workers were still finishing her when passengers arrived. The smell of wet paint and varnish, not fully cured, mingled with salt air and coal smoke. Perfection had been hurried into place, but schedules had been kept.

Titanic, Public Domain

On April 4, she docked stern-first at Berth 44 in Southampton.[1] Coal wagons rattled in, and black dust settled into seams of clothing and along the dock's edge. Cranes swung mailbags and crates aboard—meat, flour, vegetables, wine for first class, sacks of potatoes, and tins for steerage.

Men queued at the shipping office to sign articles. They were firemen, trimmers, stewards, and deckhands. Officers assigned cabins near the bridge. Then, in smaller numbers, women arrived. They came with references folded into envelopes, names already known to the company. A stewardess signed her contract and located her quarters—narrow, practical, below the deck she would patrol.

On April 10, passengers began to arrive. As they stepped from the harbor, stewardesses were already aboard. Linens were inspected, lifejackets were tallied, and cabin assignments were committed to memory. They would spend the next days carrying trays, folding blankets, directing women to promenades, and settling restless children in unfamiliar bunks. They would speak in tones that suggested everything was under control.

Stewardesses

Mary Jane "May" Sloan: Victualing Department

The record remains. Mary Jane Sloan signed onto Titanic as a stewardess, and her name appears on published crew lists as "Sloan, Miss Mary … Stewardess …" and one word added later: "saved."

When Mary Jane Sloan arrived in Southampton in the first week of April 1912, she had seen great hulls before, rising from Belfast's shipyard cranes like unfinished cathedrals. She understood better than most that magnificence is assembled piece by piece by hands rarely seen in photographs.

Born at 59 Little Patrick Street in Belfast's northern quarter, she was part of the generation of shipyard daughters who grew up with the clang of metal and the smell of coal in their lungs. The sound of hammering was as ordinary as church bells. The men of the city built ships, and the women managed the domestic worlds within them. Service was expected.

Illustration, Mary Sloan

The White Star offices in Southampton were brisk that morning, names being entered into ledgers in careful ink. Sloan, Miss Mary. Stewardess. Victualing Department. Her role placed her within the machinery of comfort. She would not stoke boilers or steer the bridge, but she would tend to the rooms that justified the ticket price, ensuring that the promise of ease held steady from embarkation to arrival.[2]

By the spring of 1912, she was forty-six years old—though that was not the story she offered on paper. On the Titanic's roster, she trimmed nearly two decades from her life, declaring herself a youthful twenty-eight. Perhaps it was vanity, or pragmatism, or simply the way working women learned to bend the truth to keep their footing in a world that rarely made room for them.

Mary had experienced trouble at sea before. She had been aboard Olympic when it collided with HMS Hawke off the Isle of Wight—an impact so violent it tore open two watertight compartments and sent passengers reeling. Yet the ship had limped back to Southampton under its own power. Mary watched it all with the calm of someone who understood the sea's moods and its willingness to remind even the largest vessels of their place. Surviving one maritime scare would have been enough to frighten off a less determined woman. But Mary Jane Sloan kept working.

When she boarded Titanic her expectations weren't of travel or reunion but of days spent in corridors where bells chimed discreetly, and doors opened onto private worlds—rooms where nervous brides adjusted their hats, widows arranged photographs on bedside tables, and mothers reassured restless children who had never slept at sea. She would memorize preferences, register anxieties, and move between decks with the quiet competence that kept class distinctions intact without drawing attention to them.

Crew quarters were narrow and practical, tucked below the passenger decks where glamour gave way to economy. Mary shared a small, furnished cabin with a locker just wide enough for a folded uniform and a few personal belongings. She unpacked deliberately: blouse pressed, apron folded, sensible shoes aligned beneath the berth. Above her, the ship was being staged.

The Forward First Class Grand Staircase of Titanic's sister ship, RMS Olympic. Titanic's staircase would have looked nearly identical. No known photos of Titanic's staircase exist.

Carpets brushed in first-class suites, and glass polished beneath the great staircase dome. Silver counted and recounted in dining saloons. Women in tailored traveling coats would soon step aboard, carrying trunks heavy with silk, letters of introduction, plans for New York apartments or Western homesteads. Electric light—steady, unblinking—glowed from chandeliers as if the nineteenth century had finally been dismissed.

In the evenings before sailing, she walked the passageways once more, learning them as a seamstress learns a pattern, tracing their logic until she could navigate them in darkness. The staircases narrowed as they rose; service corridors twisted behind paneled walls; the distance between decks was measured in both steps and status.

Maude Slocombe: Turkish Bath Attendant

Born in England in 1881, Maude Slocombe belonged to a generation of women who entered service not as temporary employment before marriage, but as a profession. Maude had worked ships before. By 1912, she was 31—older than many of the stewardesses who shared cramped quarters below deck, seasoned by years of tending to other people's comfort in spaces designed to feel effortless.[3] She knew the smell of coal mingled with soap, how steam behaved differently at sea than on land, and how condensation gathered on tile when the outside air ran cold. She understood temperature not as comfort alone, but as control. Too hot, and complaints followed. Too cool, and the illusion thinned.

When she reported to Southampton to sign her articles for Titanic, her name was entered formally: Slocombe, Mrs. Maude Louise. Turkish Bath Stewardess. Her quarters were modest; her trunk small. A working woman does not travel with excess.

Women like Maude were essential to ocean liners, though rarely spoken of in the same breath as stewards or officers. Maude's work was both physical and personal: guiding women of privilege into private rooms, adjusting the temperature of the chambers, the air smelling of perfumed oils. She offered the calm professionalism expected of a woman who encountered people at their most vulnerable and cared for them without fuss.

Maude Slocombe

Maude's authority was quiet, and she had an attendant's instinct for the rhythms of a voyage—when the crowds would arrive, when the rooms would fall silent, when a passenger's voice carried a weariness that needed tending.

She recognized when a patron wished to speak and when silence was preferred. Service at that level required reading not only instructions but temperament.

When she signed on to Titanic, she stepped into the largest, most luxurious environment she had ever worked in. The Turkish baths on this ship were unlike anything afloat—fit for royalty, it was said. It was a place meant to soften the edges of travel, making the passage feel like indulgence rather than endurance. A bath on land must be warm. A bath at sea must be flawless. Women arrived to rest, to converse in softened air, and to maintain routine in transit. A crossing of nearly a week could unsettle the body. Steam and ritual steadied it. The Atlantic might rage unseen outside steel walls, but inside tile and marble, civilization held.

Before the passengers arrived, she inspected the bath complex carefully. The tiled frigidarium and tepidarium. The steam room chamber. Marble slabs were scrubbed until they reflected light. Brass fittings polished, towels counted and stacked. Slippers paired. She adjusted valves, monitored moisture, and ensured privacy. Above her, carpenters were tightening screws in first-class suites. Below, firemen were preparing furnaces that would power the ship's enormous boilers. Titanic was layered industry disguised as serenity.

On the afternoon Titanic prepared to sail, she would have stood for a moment in the doorway of the baths, assessing light against tile, steam rising in measured curls, and allowed herself the small satisfaction of completion. The room was ready. The illusion intact.

She had likely already known compromise; an unmarried woman her age in Edwardian England had navigated a world not built for her independence. Work granted her both wages and standing. She believed she understood the sea, ships, and the work. But nothing in her years of tending to travelers could have prepared her for how swiftly the world aboard Titanic would change.

Passengers

First Class: Helen Churchill Candee

First-class women stepped up the gangway in tailored coats and high-collared blouses, trunks trailing behind. The crossing promised leisure—dinners, promenades, the slow passage between continents.

But for one passenger, it was something else entirely. Helen Churchill Candee boarded with urgency folded into her ticket. A telegram had reached her in Paris: her son had been badly injured. The voyage that others treated as indulgence became, for her, a straight line across the Atlantic.

She was not new to making her own way. Years earlier, she had written a best-selling book, *How Women May Earn a Living,* a blunt, practical guide for women trying to stand upright in a world that preferred them seated. That mattered here, on a ship engineered to flatter dependence.

Helen knew what it meant to rebuild a life from splintered pieces. She had married young, as so many women of her generation did, stepping into a role society had rehearsed for her long before she arrived. But for her, marriage did not unfold as the storybooks promised.

Edward Candee's temper darkened the home, and later, when he abandoned the family, Helen was left with two children and a future suddenly stripped of guarantees.

In the long shadow of that departure, she discovered what women were seldom encouraged to admit: survival is a craft. Helen learned to shape hers with a pen. She sold articles to Scribner's and The Ladies' Home Journal, writing first about the domestic sphere she was expected to inhabit—manners, housekeeping, the quiet economies of mothering. She published widely on design, decoration, and tapestry, bringing her aesthetic sensibilities to a national audience through books and magazines.

Helen Churchill Candee

Yet her curiosity stretched far beyond parlor walls. She wrote about education, child-rearing, and eventually the precarious balancing act women performed when society offered them responsibility without independence.[4]

By now, she was a familiar name in Washington society—a woman whose movements were noted in the newspapers and whose dinner parties drew diplomats, writers, and political figures alike. Her keen eye and impeccable taste quickly won her admirers. President Theodore Roosevelt sought her counsel, as did Nathan Wyeth, the architect of the Oval Office, who consulted her on the design and decoration of the West Wing. What began as personal artistry became professional influence: Helen transformed herself into one of the earliest successful female interior decorators in the capital.

Helen's life blended intellect, resilience, and social grace—a combination that made her both admired and notable in an era when women's voices were still fighting to be heard.

It was this same poised, capable woman who stepped aboard Titanic in April 1912—resourceful, independent, and accustomed to navigating the world on her own terms. She had survived abandonment, built a career in a world reluctant to make space for women, and fashioned a public voice that pushed against the edges of expectation. Helen had already learned that reinvention was its own kind of voyage. Yet beneath these accomplishments was a truth she rarely spoke of: survival, for women like her, was rarely granted—only earned.

She arrived at her cabin, feeling the tug of urgency, a mother's instinct pulling her toward home like a compass set to true north. If the ship held its course and the weather stayed kind, she would soon be home. But worry had a way of keeping step.

Inside the cabin, sunlight pushed through the porthole in a bright oval, casting a warm glow over the upholstered chairs and the neatly folded coverlet. She set down her valise, smoothed the travel wrinkles from her skirt, and felt the faint hum of the engines underfoot. The ship was alive, and soon the coastline would drop behind them, leaving nothing but water and waiting. And for the first time since receiving the cable about her son, she felt a faint thread of hope pull taut.

First Class: Edith Rosenbaum

Edith Rosenbaum did not board at Southampton, where the great ship first exhaled smoke and ceremony. She arrived later, under a lowering sky at Cherbourg. From the small boat ferrying first-class passengers out to the anchored liner, Titanic must have seemed less like transportation and more like architecture. Steel rising from the water, with lighted portholes already aglow in the early evening. A city waiting offshore.

She was traveling not as a tourist but as a professional woman in transit between worlds. Her career was unusual and glamorous: she was a fashion correspondent for *Women's Wear Daily* and a buyer who moved between Paris and New York, carrying trunks full of new garments that had to arrive intact, on time, and uncrushed across the Atlantic.[5]

The Paris fittings and negotiations conducted in mirrored rooms were behind her. New York was ahead—buyers, deadlines, and expectations. Her 19 trunks followed. So did the weight of what they contained: a season's worth of fabric and pattern.

She had spent the early days of April in the whirring rhythm of Paris fashion and had intended to return to New York on the steamship George Washington, scheduled to sail on Easter Sunday. But a cable from her editor arrived with an assignment to cover the Paris–Roubaix race on Sunday. It was not a request but a command for a correspondent who had fought for her place in a field where women were still treated as a novelty. So she unpacked what she had packed, rearranged her plans, and booked passage on the next practical crossing. That ship was RMS Titanic.

A steward directed her along polished corridors. Her ticket was £27, roughly $4,500 today, and it granted her cabin A-11 on the promenade deck. The room was spacious, with a bell pull by the bed and a mirror framed in intricately carved wood. She brought with her cases of notes, a few prized garments, and the talismanic possessions she never traveled without.

In her own account, she describes having a large cabin on the promenade deck and — immediately opposite — another of the same type for her luggage.

Room enough for a woman accustomed to display. Not indulgence, exactly, but insurance. After all, fashion did not travel lightly. Silk bruised, hats collapsed, and embroidery snagged on careless corners. The ocean had no sympathy for couture. If she required two cabins, it was because the cargo demanded it. The Atlantic could be trusted with steam and steel, but garments required something more controlled.

Edith Rosenbaum

40

The arrangement reflected the rules of her world. She would have space between sleeping quarters and storage, between herself and the merchandise. It was manageable if one had the means. In the corridors outside, other first-class women were arriving. They unbuttoned their coats, removed their gloves, and exchanged greetings. Their accents carried capital and lineage. The ship absorbed them all without visible strain.

Edith would later write of a premonition, a sense that had nearly made her cancel the crossing. But on that first evening, the ship offered no warning. The trunks were placed carefully. The door closed. The Atlantic waited beyond the glass.

Second Class, Brown Family: Elizabeth and Edith Brown

The Brown family did not board Titanic with trunks full of gowns or suitcases filled with luxury. They boarded with subtraction.

From their home in South Africa, 1912 had arrived with more worry than promise. The economy had thinned around them like worn fabric. The United States held better prospects than South Africa, and if they wanted opportunity, they would have to cross an ocean to find it. The family had sold what they could not carry. Seattle waited with the blunt promise of timber and rain.

Edith's father secured tickets for the crossing: joint ticket number 29750, second class. The cost—£39—was no small sum for a family reevaluating its footing, but it bought them passage on a ship the entire world was talking about.[6] Even so, the class of travel disappointed Edith's mother.

She had been raised on the comforts of first class—the
polish of attentive service, the soft certainty of linen and
crystal—and she felt the downgrade personally.

Edith Brown

Edith, though, saw none of that. She was sixteen, bright-
eyed, and unburdened by the scale of adult expectations.
Stepping onto Titanic for the first time, she was struck by
the ship's grandeur, its opulent radiance unfolding like a
fairy tale. Even in second class, the accommodations
impressed her. She admired the framed prints on the walls,
the delicate tableware set out with practiced precision, the
linens folded so crisply that they seemed to promise a
better life simply by touching them.

Edith took it all in with wide, earnest wonder. Later, she would recall every detail: the gleam of the fixtures, the quality of the meals, the unexpected luxury tucked into every corner of second class.

As Titanic pulled away from Southampton, they could not guess how profoundly the days ahead would alter the story they thought they were stepping into.

Second Class, Elizabeth Mellenger

Elizabeth Mellenger boarded Titanic not as a wife and mother, but as a woman in the space just after. Divorce in 1912 did not simply dissolve a marriage; it rearranged a woman's standing in the world. It altered how she was spoken to, how she was regarded at a ticket counter, and even how her luggage was labeled. A married woman traveled under her husband's protection. A divorced woman traveled under her own.

The previous year, she had reached the breaking point in her life. Elizabeth, once at the center of a bustling household, now appeared in census records as a "married domestic," living not with her children but under the roof of the Carpenter sisters at 4 Old Field Road in Wimbledon, England. Her husband had slipped out of their lives, leaving absence in his place, and the responsibility for five children had fractured under the weight of her circumstances.

The census pages tell the rest of the story with cruel precision. Her son, Alexander, was listed as an inmate at Gordon's Boys Home in Chobham, earning what he could as a part-time carpenter. Her daughter, Madeline, appeared at a children's home on Worple Road. The whereabouts of the two youngest children remained uncertain—silent spaces in the record that spoke louder than any entry. The grief was not only separation but also the indignity of having one's private struggles laid bare in ink.

Recreation, Violet Mellenger

Her divorce in that era had required both courage and calculation. It meant choosing instability and accepting that security would now be earned weekly rather than promised indefinitely. Elizabeth was now bound for Vermont, not to join society but to enter service. Early in 1912, she seized an opportunity thousands of miles away: a position as housekeeper at Fillmore Farms in Bennington, Vermont, part of the Colgate family estate—the same family whose name drifted through American households on pink-striped toothpaste boxes. It was respectable work that offered something her life had lately lacked: stability and the faint outline of a future she might rebuild.

She took her daughter, Violet, with her, the bright-eyed child who had stayed closest through the unraveling of their family. When the time came, the two boarded Titanic at Southampton on the morning of 10 April 1912, traveling second class on ticket 250644. The fare—£19 and 10 shillings—was a stretch.[7]

She carried fewer trunks than some. Her belongings would have fit neatly into a small cabin: work-appropriate dresses, perhaps one kept aside for Sundays. Letters folded into envelopes with addresses written carefully in ink. On deck, she might have stood alone more often than the married women. Divorce marks a woman quietly; she learns to hold her own posture.

Second class carried people like her—respectable but in transition. The deck between display and density. A dining saloon, bright and orderly, with polished cutlery and upright chairs close together. No orchestra, but no shame either. She understood hierarchy intimately. Which staircases you may use, which spaces belong to other women, and which belong to you. It was a narrow middle rung—a place for teachers, clerks, widows, and women who had counted carefully before stepping forward. Their cabins were clean and orderly, polished but plain. A washbasin and hooks for coats. Enough space to turn without touching the walls.

There was no going back now, only onward across the wide Atlantic toward a future she was determined to claim.

For Violet, the ship was a marvel: the noise of the winches, the gleam of the brass, the vast sweep of the decks that felt like an entire world suspended above the sea. The Atlantic in April was cold and clear. The wind off the water stung the cheeks and sharpened the senses.

Around her, conversations rose and fell—businessmen discussing markets, families speaking of reunions, and children darting between deck chairs. She had chosen motion over stillness. The sea, for the moment, agreed.

Third Class: Rhoda Abbott

Rhoda Abbott boarded Titanic with trunks and with boys. Two sons—Rossmore and Eugene, aged 16 and 13—old enough to stand tall beside her, young enough to still be guided by her hand in unfamiliar corridors.[8] They were her future compressed into narrow passageways.

By the spring of 1911, Rhoda Abbott had already weathered more upheaval than most women her age. Newly divorced—a condition society still treated as a moral bruise—she gathered her two sons and left Rhode Island for England, crossing on the RMS Olympic. In Southampton, she stitched together a living as a seamstress, her days marked by the rhythm of needle and thread, the quiet industry of a woman determined to provide for her children.

But it did not take long for her to see that England was shrinking around the boys. They missed America—the open spaces, the familiar voices, the sense of belonging they had once taken for granted. The gray English skies, the small rented rooms, and the constant scrimping all wore on them in ways Rhoda could not ignore. So she made a decision that required all the courage she had honed through hardship: they would go back. Back to the country where possibilities still seemed plentiful, where her sons might grow into themselves instead of bending to circumstance. She booked their passage for April 1912, counting the coins, measuring the risks, and believing— because she had to—that the journey would lead them toward something better.

On the morning of 10 April, the trio boarded RMS Titanic at Southampton as third-class passengers. The ship towered above them, its sheer size enough to make the boys forget their worries for a moment. Their quarters were modest—no brass fittings or fine linens here—but to Rhoda it was enough. A bunk, a berth, and a ticket home. Third class lay deep within the ship's body. Cabins were compact, arranged in practical rows along corridors that hummed faintly with machinery.

For many immigrants, Titanic was a modern crossing. But modern did not mean accessible. To reach the open deck from steerage required ascending staircases that narrowed and passing through corridors designed for control. Gates regulated movement between classes, partly for health-inspection compliance and partly to maintain order.

Rhoda Abbott, Public Domain

Rhoda would have learned the geography quickly. Which staircase turned where, which corridor led toward light. A mother memorizes exits the way she memorizes faces. Her sons would have roamed within permitted limits, testing boundaries, and peering at the bright world above. Rossmore at sixteen would have been nearly a man—tall, restless, curious about machinery and the wide decks above. Eugene, younger, likely followed him closely. Boys that age are drawn toward railings, toward engines, toward any place that vibrates with motion.

Steerage carried hope differently than first class. It carried it in bundles and rationed portions. In children's boots and women's shawls, and in the quiet resolve of those who had spent their last coins on passage. For now, Rhoda was simply a mother at sea, keeping her sons close and believing—as they all did—that arrival waited somewhere beyond the horizon.

Third Class: Leah Aks

Leah Aks was eighteen years old when she boarded Titanic at Southampton on April 10, 1912. She was traveling alone with her 10-month-old infant son. His name was Philip Franklin, though she called him "Filly."

Leah had been born Leah Rosen in Poland, then part of the Russian Empire. She grew up in a world of tight streets and tighter restrictions, where Jewish families navigated both poverty and periodic violence. By the time she reached her twenties, the pattern was familiar across Eastern Europe: men left first, seeking work in America; wives followed when money allowed.

When Sam Aks left in January 1912, he had sailed from Liverpool to New York aboard the Cymric, hoping the promise of American wages might outweigh the loneliness of separation. A tailor by trade, he found work and saved money in Norfolk, Virginia. By 1912, he had secured enough funds to purchase two third-class tickets.[9]

Samuel, Phillip and Leah Aks

At first, Leah planned to sail earlier. But, as family accounts say, her mother persuaded her to wait one more week and travel on the new White Star liner—the Titanic—advertised as the world's safest ship. Its reputation, its size, and its modernity all seemed to promise a secure passage. Leah agreed, packed their few belongings, and on the morning of April 10, 1912, she carried her son up Titanic's gangway at Southampton.

She boarded with a small valise, a bundle of clothing, and a child who could not walk but could cry loudly. Her third-class ticket—number 392091, costing £9 and 7 shillings—was tucked safely away, granting her and Filly a cabin to themselves, a small blessing on a ship crowded with so many emigrants. It was a modest berth, a modest fare, but to Leah it represented everything she had hoped for: reunion, security, and the possibility of a new life stitched together in the fabric of America. Language also shaped her experience. Many steerage passengers spoke little English and, like Leah, would have navigated the ship in Yiddish and gestures. Instructions from the crew filtered down unevenly. Trust traveled through tone as much as through words. But that would come later.

Her luggage was built for endurance, not display—scuffed trunks, canvas bags, wooden boxes hammered together in kitchens and sheds. Inside them lay the pared-down essentials of a future: work clothes, family papers, and the few cherished objects that survived the calculus of departure.

In first class, luggage announced one's fortune. In steerage, it revealed one's survival strategy. And long after the night the ship went down, the retrieved trunks and suitcases told their own quiet stories. Raised from the seabed, they opened onto the small, stubborn details of interrupted lives—tools polished from use, neatly folded clothes, family documents inked with hopes that never reached America.

Leah was young, tired, and hopeful. The fear of traveling alone with a baby was softened by the image of Sam waiting across the vast ocean, ready to begin their lives again.

On the morning of April 10, 1912, the lines were
confidently cast off, and the Atlantic stretched wide and
indifferent before the bow. And every woman aboard—
whether in silk, wool, or uniform—stepped into that
confidence believing the Atlantic would part cleanly ahead.
Titanic carried them all—steadily, confidently, its engines
pressing forward through water that seemed to part
willingly. The decks vibrated with assurance. The lights
burned without flicker. Nothing about the voyage
suggested it would be interrupted in a single, almost polite
shudder of steel.

Titanic leaving Southampton

[1] Eaton, John P.; Haas, Charles A. (1995). Titanic: Triumph and Tragedy. New York: W.W. Norton & Company.

[2] Titanic Belfast. "A History of the Shipyard: The People of Belfast."

[3] Mark Chirnside et al., "Maude Louise Slocombe – Titanic Survivor."

[4] Biographical Cyclopedia of U.S. Women (1924).

[5] Brewster, Hugh (2013). RMS Titanic : Gilded Lives on a Fatal Voyage (1st ed.). Toronto: Collins.

[6] Butler, Daniel Allen (1998). Unsinkable: the full story of the RMS Titanic (1st ed.). Mechanicsburg, PA.

[7] Encyclopedia Titanica. "Mrs. Elizabeth Anne Mellenger (née Maidment)."

[8] Mrs Rhoda Mary 'Rosa' Abbott (née Hunt)". Encyclopedia Titanica.

[9] Encyclopedia Titanica. "Mrs. Leah Aks (née Rosen)."

Part II — The Voyage Begins

Chapter 3 — Underway

The sea, once it casts its spell, holds one in its net of wonder forever.

— Jacques-Yves Cousteau

AT 11:45 A.M. ON April 10, 1912, as the last lines were cast off and tugboats nudged her away from the quay, Titanic's deep steam whistles rolled across Southampton harbor. She moved with the slow, deliberate confidence of a vessel built to impress, sliding down Southampton Water on the first miles of her maiden voyage to New York. But the departure did not go smoothly.

Just minutes after clearing the dock, Titanic passed the moored liners SS City of New York and Oceanic. The sheer mass of the new ship pushed a swell ahead of her, lifting the smaller vessels and then dropping them sharply into the trough behind. New York's mooring lines, already taut, snapped under the sudden strain. In an instant, the ship swung stern-first toward Titanic, drifting fast and far too close.

The tug Vulcan rushed in, struggling to take New York under tow, while Captain Smith ordered Titanic's engines "full astern." Crew and onlookers held their breath as the gap narrowed—four feet was all that ultimately remained between the two hulls. It was a near miss so dramatic that it brought passengers to the rails and left harbor officials stunned.[1]

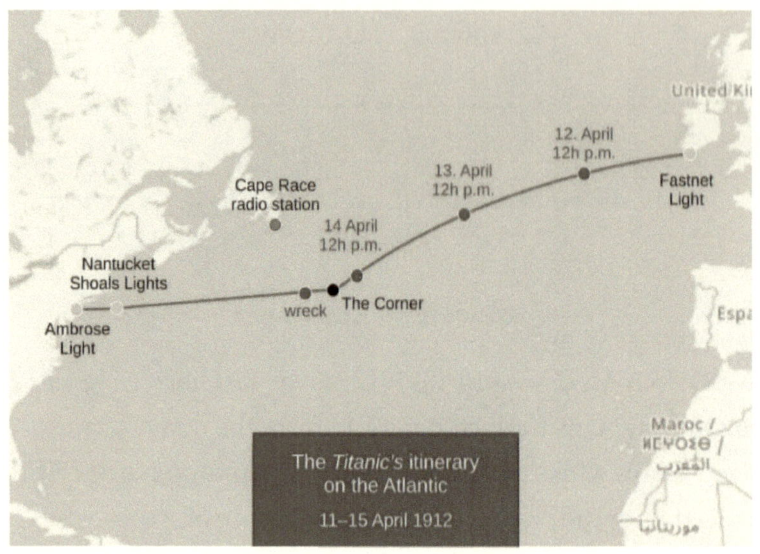

The *Titanic's* itinerary
on the Atlantic

11–15 April 1912

The incident set the great liner's schedule back by an
hour while New York was secured and brought under
control. But by a little after 1 p.m., Titanic gathered herself
and pushed onward, her bows turning toward the open
sea. Behind her, the harbor settled back into calm, the
narrow escape already slipping into the background of a
voyage the world believed unsinkable. Ahead lay the
Atlantic, and a crossing no one would ever forget.

The Lives on Board

In total, 920 passengers boarded Titanic at Southampton:
179 in First Class, 247 in Second Class, and 494 in Third
Class. Additional passengers were taken aboard at
Cherbourg and Queenstown.

While passenger lists reduce individuals to categories:
age, sex, occupation, nationality, and class, they miss the
humanity of the people behind the statistics, who carried
the quiet courage of leaving everything familiar behind.

Walking the decks, they felt the vibrations of engines beneath polished floors. They smelled coal smoke mingled with drying paint. They admired the detail, the care, and the argument the ship made about modernity. Few would have studied the lifeboats.

They hung in neat rows, sufficient by the standards of regulation, insufficient by the arithmetic of total bodies. After all, Titanic was built to display mastery over the ocean and class itself. She promised that luxury could float, that order could be engineered, that risk could be managed through design. For four days, the Atlantic accepted that promise.

The First Days at Sea

For the first-class passengers, the opening days of the voyage were a soft glide into routine—the ship settling around them like a well-tailored coat. The Atlantic stayed calm, the sky clear, and Titanic moved with a steadiness that made even seasoned travelers remark on her grace. For women like Edith Rosenbaum and Helen Candee, the rhythm of life aboard the ship quickly took shape.

Helen Churchill Candee was not entirely alone when she stepped aboard Titanic: she entered the voyage already woven into a small, familiar circle from Washington. On board were Major Archibald Butt and Francis Millet for dinner—old friends from D.C., and men whose company she valued for their intelligence, wit, and steady presence. Butt, crisp in manner and meticulously courteous, carried with him the unmistakable air of a man accustomed to navigating power. Millet, the painter and writer, brought a gentler warmth to the table, his conversation drifting easily from art to politics to the little absurdities of life at sea.

Titanic passenger looking out to sea, Lifeboats visible in the background.

They dined together regularly, the clink of cutlery punctuating the easy rhythm of their conversation. Helen listened, contributed, observed—always observing. These men were part of her world back home, and their presence made the wide Atlantic feel a shade smaller.

During the first days of the voyage, she also became acquainted with two other first-class passengers: Edward Kent, the architect whose measured voice and thoughtful demeanor she found immediately appealing, and Hugh Woolner, the Englishman with a keen sense of humor and a knack for turning even casual conversation into lively entertainment. They were not close friends yet, but Helen was the sort of woman who moved naturally among

60

people, forming connections with the same grace she brought to her writing and her work in Washington.

She quickly adopted a routine. Mornings found her walking the Promenade Deck, her stride brisk; her gloved hands clasped behind her back as she admired the glittering seam between sky and sea. She had always paid attention to detail—journalists must—and she noticed the little things: the hum of conversation among fellow travelers, and the way the sunlight caught on the brass railings.

First Class Dining Saloon, Titanic, Public Domain

After luncheon, she often retreated to the writing room, where the clerks knew her by her tidy handwriting and the speed with which she filled a page. There, she sent notes, drafted letters, and tried to collect her thoughts. In her 1912 narrative account of the voyage, published shortly after the disaster, she recalled feeling a sudden sense of foreboding

when she boarded the ship. She wrote that the feeling was
strong enough that she almost abandoned the trip and even
contacted her secretary.[2]

*"Arriving in Cherbourg, my premonition of ill was so strong that
again I was tempted not to take the trip, and even telegraphed my
secretary expressing my fears."*

But for now, the ship's elegance pressed in around her—
soft carpets, polished tables, the hush of other women
reading or writing. Her focus remained on the future,
counting the days until she would be home.

Edith Rosenbaum, by contrast, moved through these
early days with the restless energy of a reporter whose eye
never stops working. The ship was full of fashion—fabrics,
silhouettes, hats trimmed in velvet or ribbon—and Edith
observed them all with the same practiced gaze accustomed
to her craft. She drifted easily through first-class spaces,
chatting with fellow passengers, noting the interplay of
colors in the dining saloon, the cut of a gown glimpsed
during afternoon tea.

In spare moments, she sometimes visited her luggage
stateroom to sort through the garments and parcels that
represented her spring season's work. These were the
treasures meant for New York—fabrics chosen in Paris,
details she intended to report on as soon as she reached the
newsroom. Her days were threaded with anticipation, not
only for arrival but for the familiar machinery of deadlines
and copy that awaited her on the other side of the Atlantic.

In the evenings, both women joined the orchestral
evenings in the first-class reception rooms, where the music

floated like warm light across the polished woodwork. They listened, conversed, or simply watched the easy pleasures of ocean travel unfold around them. For the first three days, the sea remained gentle, the weather fair, and Titanic gave every impression of keeping her promises.

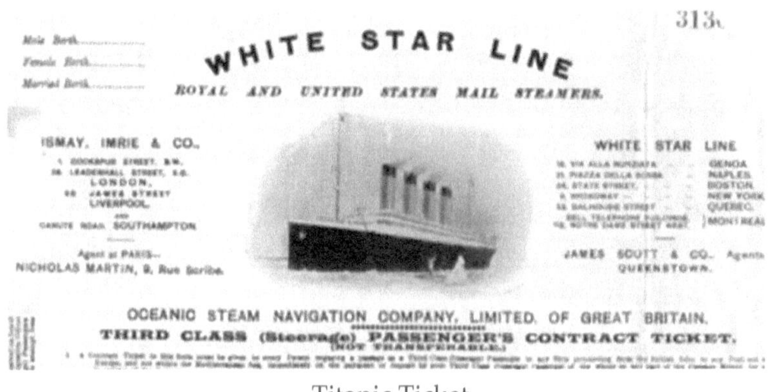

Titanic Ticket

In second class, the early days of the voyage carried a different rhythm—less opulent than first class, but comfortable in a way that felt almost luxurious to those who had known harder years. Titanic's second-class decks were bright with promise, where attentive stewards served hot meals on china that gleamed under the dining-saloon lamps. For families like the Browns, and for women like Elizabeth Mellenger and her daughter Violet, the first three days at sea unfolded with a mix of wonder, relief, and the quiet work of adjusting to life between two continents.

For the Brown family, the days before the collision passed in a pleasant rhythm of meals, walks, and the unexpected friendships that bloom easily aboard a long sea crossing. They were sociable people by nature, and Titanic's second-class community offered no shortage of company. During the voyage they grew acquainted with

William H. Harbeck, the Canadian filmmaker who carried his camera everywhere, capturing the world as he moved through it. They also came to know Reverend Carter and his wife Lillian—steady, warm companions whose conversations helped occupy the long afternoons at sea.

Edith, who was just sixteen, found these interactions thrilling. She was stepping into a world bigger than the one she had left behind in South Africa, and she absorbed every detail with wide-eyed curiosity. She spent the first mornings pressed against the railings, watching the sea slip by in endless dark-blue sheets. She traced the outlines of the ship with her eyes—its towering funnels, its endless corridors—and marveled that even as second-class passengers they were surrounded by comforts she could not have imagined back home.

One of her sharpest memories—recounted years later— was being introduced to First Officer William Murdoch during a guided tour of the bridge. The officers were proud to show off the newest and grandest ship afloat, and Edith remembered Murdoch's politeness, his calm, capable manner, and the confidence with which he seemed to inhabit the command he helped share.

Another memory stayed with her for different reasons. Edith met a woman traveling with her husband and young daughter, a woman clearly uneasy about the sea. She had never been on a ship before, and the vastness of the Atlantic only deepened her anxiety. Edith recalled trying to soothe her fears, though she admitted in later years she could not remember the family's name. With hindsight, the details matched only one possibility: Esther Hart, traveling with her husband Benjamin and their seven-year-old daughter, Eva. At the time, Edith had no way of knowing what would become of them after the collision. Later in life, on the Titanic lecture circuit, Edith and Eva Hart would meet again—two survivors, each carrying their own version of that night, recognizing in the other a link to the same vanished world.

Her mother, Elizabeth, carried herself with more restraint. The accommodations were respectable, even lovely in places, but she was accustomed to even grander surroundings. She smoothed the linens, checked the meals, and kept an eye on the service with the practiced vigilance of someone who had once expected more. And yet, even she found moments of quiet pleasure: tea in the library, a walk on deck when the wind died down, the restful hum of the engines below. For both mother and daughter, the voyage felt like the beginning of a new chapter, each sunrise carrying them closer to the promise of America.

For the Browns, those early days at sea felt safe and full of promise. They could not know that the names and faces they had just learned—Harbeck, the Carters, Murdoch, the anxious young mother—would soon become part of a story remembered not for the voyage, but for the tragedy waiting in the dark ahead.

Elizabeth Mellenger and her daughter Violet moved through these early days with a different kind of gratitude—quieter, deeper, rooted in hardship. After years of separation from her children and a life pared down to survival, Elizabeth found the ship's

Titanic Gymnasium

orderliness almost startling. She embraced the security of
the small second-class cabin, and the meals, predictable and
warm, felt like kindness. Violet, wide-eyed and eager,
explored every corner she was allowed to enter.

She lingered near the railings, fascinated by the way the wind lifted strands of her hair, by the long sweep of waves stretching toward the horizon. To her, the ship was a floating city, full of stairways and other families speaking languages she had never heard. Elizabeth spent her time studying the American families aboard, imagining the life she hoped to build on the Colgate estate in Vermont— steady work, regular wages, and perhaps, at last, a home that belonged to her and her daughter.

Every afternoon between one and three, Titanic's gymnasium opened its doors to the youngest passengers— two bright hours when the rules relaxed, the polished equipment became playgrounds, and the ship felt less like a vessel of strict routines and more like a floating adventure. For second-class families, whose children had fewer extravagances in their daily lives, the gymnasium was a marvel: all steel, leather, and ingenuity, humming faintly with the electricity that powered its machines. Violet Mellenger and Edith Brown stood in the doorway, with light pouring in from the promenade windows and shining across the gleaming rowing machines, the mechanical horse and camel, and the whirring bicycle apparatus that fascinated every child who saw it.

A kindly attendant waved them in, and they tried the rowing machine, gripping the handles with a serious grip as the levers clacked and slid. The room was noisy in the best possible way: children calling for turns, the soft thunk of wooden pedals, the mechanical whir of bicycle wheels spinning in place. Mothers lingered at the edges, talking in low, tired voices, grateful for a rare hour when their children were both safe and entertained.

For families who had left behind uncertainty—economic hardship, broken households, countries that no longer felt like home—these afternoons brought a rare sense of ease. The great ship, with all its engines and steel, had somehow made space for joy.

Meals were the anchor of the day for both families. In the dining saloon, waiters moved with quiet ceremony, and the courses arrived as though the ship itself wished to welcome them. Second-class dining offered soups, roasts, potatoes, puddings—simple dishes compared to first class, but well-prepared and served with a civility that reminded passengers they were valued. In those first days, the sea remained calm. The decks were filled with families strolling in the clear air, children chasing one another between rows of benches, women settling into the routines of the voyage.

In third class, life aboard Titanic unfolded with a blend of noise, closeness, and simple comfort. The accommodations were modest—shared spaces and long corridors echoing with many languages—but for immigrant families used to hardship, the ship felt almost generous.

Rhoda Abbott moved through these early days with the quiet vigilance of a single mother accustomed to holding her world together by sheer will. Her two boys, Eugene and Rossmore, were quick to find their footing in the lively third-class community. On the first afternoon, they joined other children in the open spaces near the stern, where the wind was sharp and laughter sharper. They chased each

other between the benches, darted around older
passengers, and leaned over the railings to watch the white
churn of the wake.

Recreation, Third-class Common Room

Rhoda allowed herself small moments of rest as she
watched them—her back against the railing, her hands still,
eyes softening. The meals were simple but comforting:
stews, bread, porridge, plates of ham and potatoes.

In the early days of the voyage, steerage passengers
gathered in common rooms. They sang and played cards.
They spoke in accents braided from across Europe. The
Atlantic stretched wide and unbroken beyond the hull, but
below deck, life felt contained, almost communal. Evenings
in third class were lively—the hum of conversation, the
occasional fiddle or harmonica, as children drifted to sleep
on laps or against tired shoulders. Rhoda often sat close to
her boys, listening but not joining in, grateful for the
warmth of community.

Across the third-class decks, Leah Aks navigated the voyage with an infant in her arms. Filly clung to her, wide-eyed and restless, unused to the motion of the sea. She walked the corridors, swaying gently, whispering in the soft cadence of Yiddish to calm him. Other women smiled at her in passing—mothers recognizing mothers, regardless of language, and admiring him for his bright eyes and small boots. Babies draw community even in transit.

This is the last known picture of RMS Titanic on the surface of the ocean. It was taken just after the vessel departed Queenstown.

Their cabin was cramped, but to Leah it felt like a temporary cradle, a small, safe pocket in the vast ocean. She unpacked carefully: a few shirts for the baby, a shawl, the small parcels of food she had brought out of habit and caution. They shared meals with other immigrant families,

Leah balancing Filly on her lap while trying to eat with one hand or passing him from kind stranger to stranger, giving his mother a moment of freedom. The dining saloon was loud and warm, the tables crowded with young men, families, and elderly travelers who spoke a patchwork of accents. She found comfort in the noise.

By the third day, the routine felt steady: short walks on deck when the weather wasn't too cold, shared benches where mothers traded stories, and restless sleep broken by the creak of the ship and the murmurs of nearby families. For Rhoda and her sons, for Leah and her baby, the voyage felt like a bridge—sometimes narrow, sometimes bright— linking the difficult past to a future they desperately wanted to believe in.

They did not know that the calm of those days was a fragile mercy. Nor could they imagine how sharply the night of April 14 would force them to cling to everything they loved.

<hr>

[1] Eaton, John P.; Haas, Charles A. (1987). Titanic: Destination Disaster: The Legends and the Reality. Wellingborough, UK.
[2] Helen Churchill Candee, "The Sinking of the Titanic," interview and survivor account, 1912, reproduced at Titanic Archive.

Chapter 4 — Day Four

···

Colossus, ship of the Titans, unsinkable beneath the stars,
Champagne popped too soon.

— Stewart Stafford

April 14, 1912

BY THE FOURTH DAY, Titanic had settled into itself. The novelty of departure had faded, and the small anxieties of boarding—finding cabins, learning routines, and testing boundaries—had shifted to routines. For many aboard, especially in steerage and among the crew, familiarity was a comfort. It signified that the ship was functioning as expected.

Sunday morning was bitterly cold. Most people stayed belowdecks, preferring the warmth of common areas to the open air.

At 9:12 a.m., a telegram arrived in the communications office, the first of many messages warning of ice ahead. One of the most striking came from the steamship Californian, reporting that she had stopped for the night, surrounded by heavy pack ice and large bergs scattered across the shipping lane.[1] The message was clear: the North Atlantic was crowded with hazards.

Titanic's two wireless operators received the warning, noting the position of the ice field in relation to the ship's course. But the Marconi room was overwhelmed that day—

passenger telegrams bound for Cape Race stacked up faster than they could be sent. Some ice messages were acknowledged, but not immediately carried to the officers on the bridge.

By evening, warnings had arrived from several ships, each painting the same picture of a frigid barrier stretching across Titanic's path. Yet the great liner pressed on at nearly full speed, engines turning confidently beneath her decks.

Helen Churchill Candee

Sunday afternoon, Helen Candee made her way to the forwardmost part of the ship, stepping into the bright, crisp wind that gathered at the bow. There, with only the horizon curving ahead and the long, white furrow trailing from the ship's passage, she felt the full magnitude of Titanic—its steadiness, its unimaginable strength, and its regal glide through the Atlantic. The water silently parted beneath her, spray lifting in a fine mist, and for a moment she stood as if suspended between sky and sea.

The immense decks behind her faded from thought; all she felt was the ship's effortless push forward, the deep hum of the engines below, and the remarkable sensation of traveling on the world's newest marvel straight into the vast blue future.

On Sunday evening, she encountered Kent and Woolner on the Promenade Deck, passengers strolling as though they were in a floating park. They paused to admire the calm weather and the ship's remarkable steadiness— observations offered with the polite understatement characteristic of first-class travelers. Helen joined them for a few minutes, the three standing together as the sea opened before them in a wide, uninterrupted blue.

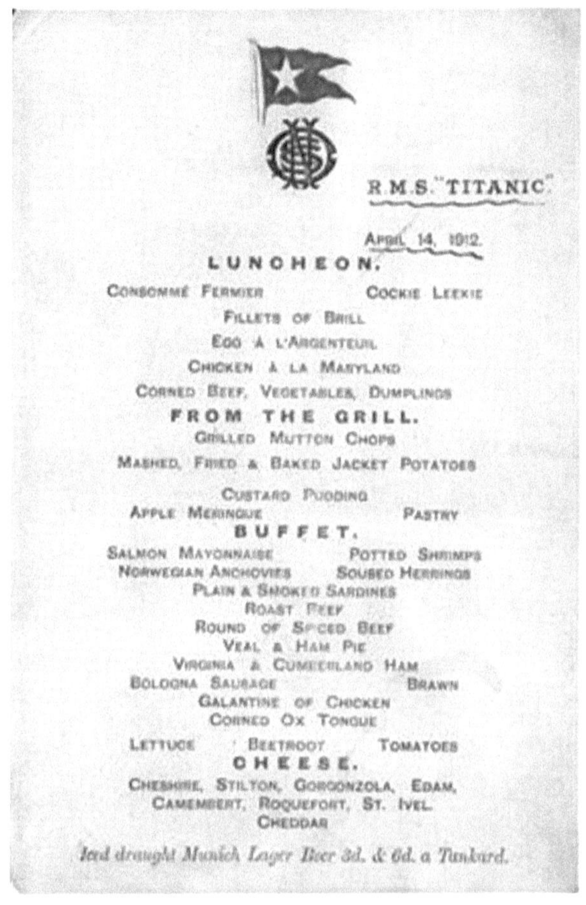

Titanic First Class Menu, April 14

Later, as she dressed for dinner, she felt a small sense of contentment she hadn't expected when she boarded. She was traveling under the strain of worry for her injured son, yet here, in this grand yet orderly world, she found herself buoyed by familiar companionship. Titanic's dining saloon—spacious, gleaming, filled with voices and the soft sweep of evening gowns—became, for a brief moment, a refuge.

Café Veranda, Starboard Side

When she parted from her friends after dinner, stepping into the quietened corridor that led toward her stateroom, Helen felt the steadiness of the ship beneath her feet and the comfort of knowing she was surrounded by people she trusted. It was a small blessing, but one she carried with her as the ship moved deeper into the cold Atlantic night.

Edith Rosenbaum

Edith Rosenbaum woke on Sunday to a gentle, rhythmic roll beneath her cabin floor. It was a steady, by now familiar motion, that made Titanic feel less like a ship and more like a grand hotel floating upon the sea. The weather had stayed clear, but cold, the decks dry, and by late morning she had settled into the pleasant routine of a crossing she had not expected to take.

First Class Promenade, Titanic

After breakfast she walked the long sweep of the first-class promenade, pausing now and then to watch the shimmer of sunlight skip across the waves. The ship moved easily and confidently. By mid-afternoon she had settled in the writing room with a stack of notes from Paris— sketches of fabrics, clippings, a few half-finished thoughts she hoped to shape into something useful once she reached New York. She wrote a little, crossed out more, and let the rest wait while she chatted with a pair of American women curious about the spring trends. Edith could never resist a conversation about fashion; the exchange left her smiling as she returned to her stateroom to change for dinner.

That evening, the dining saloon glowed under its electric lights, the hum of conversation mingling with the clink of glassware as stewards carried in the courses. Edith took her seat among the other first-class travelers, enjoying the easy civility of a ship where everyone, for a moment, lived as though the world were gentle and predictable. She ate well, laughed lightly and admired a particularly well-cut gown across the room—a Paris piece, she was sure of it.

Later, pleasantly tired, she made her way back through the quieting corridors, heels tapping softly against the carpeted floors. In her cabin, she loosened the fastenings of her dress, slipped off her embroidered shoes and folded the garments she planned to wear the next day. She placed her cherished music box on the bedside table exactly where she liked it. The engines thrummed beneath her like a distant heartbeat. She slipped into bed with the ease of someone who had traveled enough to trust the calm of an open sea.

Edith Rosenbaums shoes, worn at dinner on Sunday evening and in the lifeboat.

It was, for Edith, a simple day—unhurried, sociable, touched with the small comforts of a fine ship in fair weather. A day that felt safe. A day she had every reason to expect would be followed by another just like it.

Elizabeth and Edith Brown

Sunday morning found the Brown family settling into a rhythm that felt almost peaceful after the disarray of the past months. Edith, bright and curious, rose early and tugged her mother toward the promenade so she could watch the sunlight sweep across the surface of the Atlantic. Elizabeth allowed herself the small pleasure of strolling with her daughter beneath a wide, blue sky.

Later in the morning, the family gathered for the second-class church service, the hymns rising softly through the saloon as passengers bowed their heads. Afterward, they enjoyed a simple Sunday luncheon of roast meat, potatoes, and a warm pudding that Edith declared the best she had ever tasted at sea. The afternoon passed in quiet conversation and reading, her father stepping out occasionally for a pipe on deck while Edith found herself drawn to the window seats in the library, watching the horizon tilt gently with the ship's motion.

By evening, they dressed for dinner, joining the steady stream of families and travelers heading toward the dining saloon. When the meal ended, they lingered just long enough to enjoy a bit of music drifting from the nearby piano before returning to their cabin. It was a Sunday that felt ordinary, hopeful, and full of small comforts—exactly the kind of day they had crossed an ocean hoping to find.

For Elizabeth Mellenger and her daughter Violet, Sunday began with Violet peering out the porthole, amazed by how the light shimmered across the water. Violet chattered about America, asking questions about Vermont and about the farm where her mother had found work. They attended the second-class Sunday service, where the hymns — familiar and steady — reminded Elizabeth of the faith that had carried her through darker days.

In the afternoon, Violet discovered the small pleasures of Titanic's public rooms: a quiet corner in the library where she leafed through a book she could barely put down, and a spot by the promenade window where she watched seabirds wheel in the distance.

As the dinner bell rang, they dressed neatly and made their way to the saloon, where the evening felt warm with companionship. Afterward, they returned to their cabin, Violet sleepy from excitement, Elizabeth moved by the rare comfort of a day free from worry.

It was their first Sunday in months that felt like steadiness. A day that whispered: perhaps things really could be better across the ocean.

Rhoda Abbott

Sunday morning in third class began with a kind of cheerful disorder — doors opening and closing, children darting through corridors, the low rumble of conversation rising as families made their way toward breakfast. Rhoda Abbott roused her sons early, urging them to wash up and straighten their clothes. She wanted them to begin the day

properly, even here, even in the tight quarters of steerage.
The boys needed structure, she believed, something steady
to hold on to while everything else in their lives was
shifting.

After breakfast, Eugene and Rossmore enjoyed time on
deck before the wind grew too sharp. The weather was fair,
the sea almost startlingly calm, and Rhoda allowed it. The
boys' laughter mixed with the low thrum of the engines,
and for a moment Rhoda felt a warmth she had not known
in months: the sense that she had made the right choice to
return to America.

Third-class passengers on deck, Public Domain.

The rest of the day settled into simple rhythms. The boys
explored open spaces with other children, inventing games,
running along the deckboards, and weaving between the
knots of adults sharing stories in a half-dozen languages.
Rhoda found comfort in the company of other mothers, all

of them traveling for reasons that rarely required
explanation—work, survival, reunion, hope.

After supper, she settled them into their bunks,
smoothing the blankets with a tenderness sharpened by all
they had endured. The ship was steady, their future close
enough to imagine, and as the boys drifted into sleep,
Rhoda allowed herself a brief moment of peace. It would be
one of the last she would ever know.

Leah Aks

For Leah Aks, Sunday aboard Titanic unfolded in the
careful, clockwork rhythm of tending to an infant at sea.
Filly woke early—he always did—and she spent the first
hours carrying him through the corridor outside their
cabin, whispering softly in Yiddish as the ship stirred
awake around them. The gentle roll of the ocean made him
restless, but the warm bustle of third class seemed to calm
him: families preparing for breakfast, young men brushing
jackets, an older woman humming as she braided a young
girl's hair.

They joined the flow of passengers heading toward the
dining saloon. Meals were noisy but warm affairs—tables
crowded, bowls passed hand to hand, a chorus of accents
filling the air. She was grateful for the hot food, grateful for
the sense of community that grew naturally among people
traveling toward the same uncertain promise.
Conversations turned to America—jobs were rumored,
relatives waited, futures were imagined but not yet real.

The ship moved steadily westward, and with it, the
fragile hopes of those below decks who, for the moment,

believed the hardest part of the journey was already behind them.

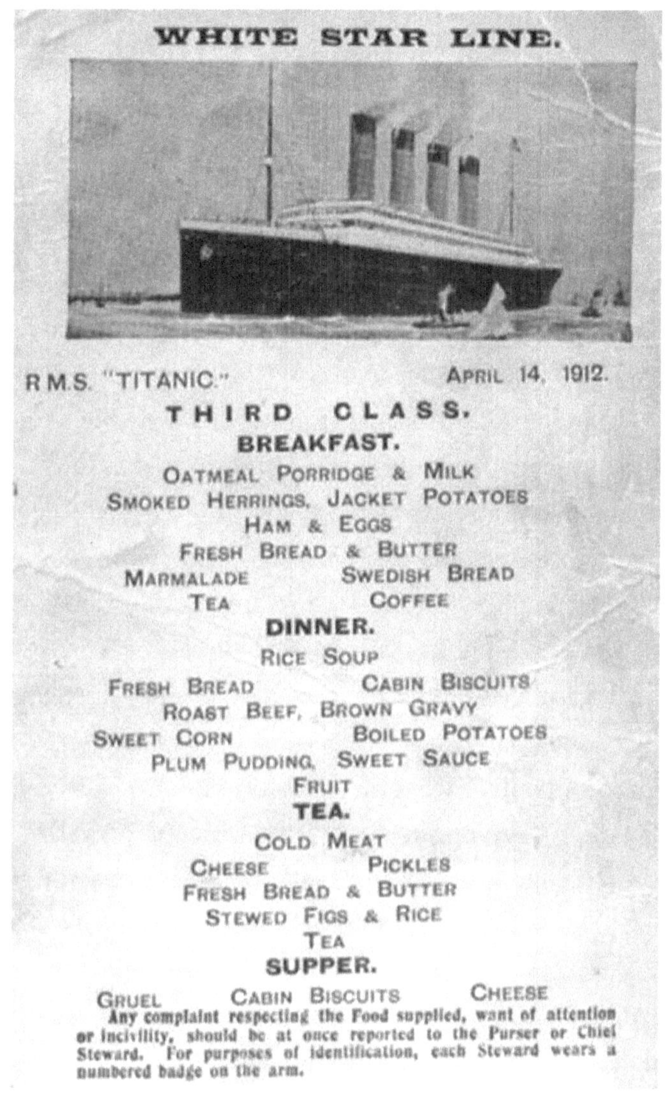

Third Class Menu, Titanic, April 14

After the evening meal, she stayed close to her cabin, humming softly as she settled Filly in for the night. The gentle motion of the Atlantic seemed — for the first time all day—to soothe them both. She used the rare stillness to organize their belongings—folding a shirt, adjusting the baby's blanket, checking the few food items she had packed from home. Leah lay down beside her son, listening to his breathing.

The Stewardesses

For the stewardesses aboard Titanic, Sunday was not a day of leisure but another full shift in the quiet machinery that kept the ship running. While passengers drifted into their routines—worship services, deck walks, long meals—the women of the stewardess corps moved through the ship with practiced precision, tending to comforts that few passengers ever paused to notice.

Maude Slocombe, working in the Turkish baths, began her morning in the warm haze of steam and tile. She laid out crisp towels, making sure the private rooms were orderly for any passengers who wanted the indulgence of a Sunday soak. The work was steady and physical, her uniform dampened by heat long before noon, but she took quiet pride in keeping the space immaculate. The baths were among Titanic's crown jewels, and even if passengers rarely knew her name, her hands helped maintain their elegance.

Above her, Mary Jane Sloan walked the corridors assigned to the stewardesses responsible for first-class cabins. A woman with years of sea service behind her, she carried herself with the no-nonsense efficiency of someone who understood ships as well as any sailor. Sunday meant fresh linens, tidying berths, collecting laundry, and seeing

that the ladies' needs were met—whether that meant
fetching hot water, offering directions to the dining saloon,
or reassuring a nervous traveler uneasy about the long
stretch of ocean still ahead.

She exchanged polite greetings as she moved from cabin
to cabin, her Belfast accent softened by years in service. She
knew the rhythm of a voyage: the early bustle, the quiet
hours of midday, the surge of activity before dinner.
Nothing on this Sunday felt unusual. The passengers were
content. The ship sailed smoothly. The officers moved with
calm confidence.

During brief moments of rest—which were few—Maude
and Mary might pass one another in a corridor or service
area, sharing a small nod of acknowledgment, the
camaraderie of women who worked hard in a world that
rarely looked in their direction. They had no illusions about
luxury. Their days were shaped by labor, not leisure, and
Sundays were no exception.

By evening, as the first-class passengers dressed for
dinner and the ship's lights glowed warm against the
darkening sea, the stewardesses finished their final rounds.
There were curtains to draw, trays to collect, last requests to
answer. When their shifts finally eased, they retreated to
the modest quarters reserved for female crew—clean, spare,
windowless—grateful for the chance to sit, to unlace their
shoes, to breathe without hurry.

They ended the day as they had begun it: steady,
unseen, essential.

For Maude Slocombe and Mary Jane Sloan, Sunday
aboard the Titanic was simply another day's work—one

more stretch of hours in a voyage that felt, at every turn, completely ordinary.

❖

By late Sunday evening, Titanic moved through the North Atlantic with a steadiness that soothed nearly everyone aboard. On the upper decks, women like Helen Candee and Edith Rosenbaum ended their day with the soft glow of electric lamps guiding them back to their rooms, the murmur of conversation fading behind them. In second class, families settled in with the same easy contentment. The Browns tucked themselves into their cabin after a peaceful Sunday spent in worship, reading, and steady sea air. Nearby, Elizabeth and Violet Mellenger prepared for bed, feeling the rare reassurance of a day without urgency.

Down in third class, the night came with a hum and shuffle of weary but satisfied travelers. Rhoda Abbott smoothed blankets over her sons, and Leah Aks curled close to her infant, soothed by the child's breathing and the comforting vibration of the ship beneath them. They believed—as so many immigrant families did—that they were being carried toward a future brighter than the one behind them.

Every part of the ship held its own version of the same truth: the voyage felt safe.

By the time the ship's clocks approached midnight, most passengers had surrendered to sleep. Only the lookouts at the bow, the officers on the bridge, and a few lingering travelers remained awake under the still, cold stars. The great liner pressed on at nearly full speed, slicing through

the dark toward the stretch of ocean where the temperature
had begun to fall.

It was the last calm night the Titanic would ever know.

The Lookout Takes His Watch

For Titanic lookout Reginald Robinson Lee, the evening of
April 14 began the way many others had—without
ceremony. At 10 p.m., he and Frederick Fleet took over
from the previous shifts watchmen.[2] In the cold, they
climbed the nearly 50 feet to the crow's nest. Frederick
stood on the port side of the crow's nest while Reginald
stood on the starboard side. High above the waterline, the
world narrowed to horizon, starlight, and darkness. From
the crow's nest, Titanic felt less like a ship and more like
motion itself—forward, steady, uninterrupted.

There was no moon. The sky was clear, the stars sharp.
The ocean lay unusually smooth, its surface offering little
contrast. The absence of binoculars—a detail later seized
upon—was not something Lee could remedy. It was not his
decision and not within his authority. And they may not
have mattered anyway. He scanned the sea as generations
of sailors had before him, relying on eyes trained to detect
shape and movement in darkness.

Below him, the ship carried thousands who had already
gone to bed. Officers maintained course. Around him, the
Atlantic offered nothing that distinguished danger from
emptiness. Minutes passed. Then more minutes. Reginald
continued to scan the horizon.

When the shape finally appeared and the night broke its silence, Reginald would do precisely what the system asked of him. He would see. He would alert.

And the rest would unfold beyond his control.

Crows Nest, Titanic

1   Walter Lord, A Night to Remember (New York: Henry Holt, 1955).
2   "Reginald Robinson Lee". Encyclopedia Titanica.

Chapter 5 – Fire and Ice

Facing it always, facing it, that's the way to get through.

— Lord Jim, 1900

Fire

BEFORE TITANIC EVER SLIPPED into open water, a quiet trouble smoldered deep within her hull. Fire.

Eight days before the ship's departure from Southampton, a coal bunker between boiler rooms 5 and 6 had begun to burn.[1] This was not a dramatic blaze—no flames licking bulkheads, no alarms ringing—just the slow, dangerous heat of a coal fire working its way inward under pressure. Such fires were an old, unwelcome companion to steamships. Coal, stored in great heaps and packed for long periods, could ignite on its own when pockets of air lingered within the mass.

A bunker fire was serious, but not serious enough to delay a maiden voyage of this scale. The remedy was the same one used on countless ships before her: attack the burning coal from within. Firemen pulled the heated clumps out, spread them to cool, and shoveled them straight into the boilers to burn away the hazard entirely. It was practical, effective—and exhausting. It demanded men to labor longer, harder, and in hotter conditions than usual, and it meant the fire would be managed steadily over time, not extinguished in a single effort.

Titanic before leaving Southampton; the circled area contains a dark area believed to be the fire in the coal bunker. Public Domain.

The Firemen at Work

According to fireman Frederick Barrett, shortly after Titanic left Southampton, he and roughly eight to ten other firemen were ordered to coal out the affected bunker in boiler room 6. Their job was simple in instruction but punishing in execution: remove the burning coal, clear the space, and keep the fire from spreading. It was the sort of work that never appeared in the glowing descriptions of Titanic's modern engineering—but it was the hidden labor that kept the great ship moving safely forward. For the men working below decks, the fire added more heat, smoke, and exhaustion to the already brutal labor. They shoveled coal in rotating shifts, in temperatures that could exceed 100 degrees.

The work of clearing the burning coal went on for days. According to later testimony from fireman Frederick Barrett, the effort did not end until Saturday, April 13—three days into the voyage. When the bunker was finally emptied enough for a close inspection, Barrett described the bulkhead as scorched from top to bottom, its steel warped by the sustained heat: the lower section pushed aft, the upper section bowed forward.

Historians continue to debate what role, if any, this damage played in the ship's final hours. But its presence tells us something essential: Titanic's maiden voyage began already under strain. The fire meant the ship's industrial heart was stressed before she ever encountered ice. It meant that below decks, long before the collision, men were laboring in conditions far harsher than the world above them ever saw.

And when the collision came—sudden, violent, transforming routine into crisis—those same men, already exhausted and overheated from days of firefighting, were the ones expected to return to the boilers, to the pumps, to the flooded compartments, and to fight again.

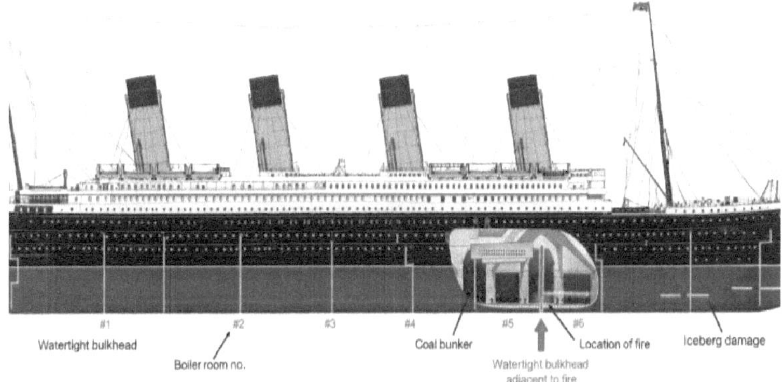

Diagram of coal bunker fire and Iceberg damage

Ice

The first sign of danger had started to arrive on the
morning of April 14, 1912., when the wireless room
received a message from the RMS Caronia: reports of
"bergs, growlers, and field ice" drifting in their path.[2]
Captain Edward J. Smith read the warning carefully,
acknowledged it, and pressed on. The North Atlantic could
be treacherous in spring, but ice reports were familiar
enough; a seasoned captain could navigate through them
safely—or so it seemed.

By early afternoon, the messages became more frequent
and more uneasy. At 1:42 p.m., RMS Baltic passed along a
note from the Greek steamer Athenia: she too had seen
"icebergs and large quantities of field ice." Smith again
acknowledged the report and, this time, brought it to the
attention of J. Bruce Ismay, chairman of the White Star Line,
who was enjoying the prestige of Titanic's maiden voyage.
After a brief consultation, Smith ordered a new, more
southerly course to steer clear of the worst of the ice.[3]

Only minutes later, at 1:45 p.m., another message
came—this one from the German liner SS Amerika, sailing
not far to the south. She had passed "two large icebergs."
But this warning never reached the bridge. The reason was
fateful yet straightforward: the Marconi wireless
transmitter aboard Titanic had broken down the night
before, and the two overworked radio operators, Jack
Phillips and Harold Bride, had spent the night repairing it.
In the rush to resume sending passengers' personal
messages, this vital alert was apparently overlooked or
misplaced.[4]

As evening fell, other ships continued to send warnings. At 7:30 p.m., SS Californian reported "three large bergs." At 9:40 p.m., another message arrived, this time from the SS Mesaba: "Saw much heavy pack ice and great number [of] large icebergs. Also field ice." It was, by any standard, a grave warning. But that message, too, never reached Captain Smith. Jack Phillips, buried under a backlog of private telegrams, was transmitting passenger messages to the Cape Race station in Newfoundland. Preoccupied, he set the Mesaba's warning aside.

At 10:30 p.m., Cyril Evans, the wireless operator from the Californian, sent a final, direct warning: his ship had come to a full stop, surrounded by ice fields only a few miles away. But when his message interrupted the stronger signals from Cape Race that Phillips was handling, he snapped back, "Keep out; shut up, I'm busy." Evans complied—and turned off his set for the night.

Despite the steady stream of reports, Titanic steamed ahead at 22 knots, nearly her top speed. Slowing down in icy waters was not the practice of the day; captains relied on their lookouts and the watch on the bridge to spot danger in time.

As Fifth Officer Harold Lowe later explained, "The custom was to go ahead and depend upon the lookouts... to pick up the ice in time to avoid hitting it."[5]

That night, the lookouts did their best. But the sea was glassy calm, the moon absent, and the bergs showed no white surf against the darkness—only silence, vast and cold. By the time the Titanic's crew finally saw the ice ahead, it was far too late.

Frederick saw it first. He immediately rang the crow's nest bell three times, then moved to the starboard side of the crow's nest and picked up the telephone to inform the officers on the bridge. Sixth Officer Moody picked up the phone and asked what they had seen.

"Iceberg right ahead," he replied.

"Thank you," said James.

James passed the warning directly to First Officer William Murdoch, who had the bridge. From that moment, everything moved with the speed of drilled procedure, compressed into a handful of seconds. Murdoch stepped toward the engine-order telegraphs and wheel commands, issuing orders meant to do two things at once: turn the ship and bleed off her forward momentum.

He ordered a hard turn—swinging the bow away from the danger as sharply as Titanic's size and speed would allow. Quartermaster Robert Hichens, stationed at the wheel, put the helm over at once.

At nearly the same moment, Murdoch signaled engine changes through the telegraphs. Testimony differs on whether the command was "stop," "full astern," or a sequence that combined both, but all accounts agree on the essential point: the bridge tried to check the ship's speed immediately to aid the turn.

Almost simultaneously, Murdoch also activated the system to close the watertight doors—a rapid, centralized action designed for precisely this kind of emergency. It was the ship's most important line of defense, designed to slow flooding before it could leap from one space to the next. All of this happened within a narrow window of seconds.

Frederick Barrett was on duty in boiler room 6 at 11:39 p.m. He was talking to the second engineer, John Henry Hesketh, when the red light and bells sounded, signaling the order to stop the engines. He shouted to the men in the boiler room to shut the dampers and the doors to the furnaces, and to shut off the wind for the fires.[6]

Impact

Then came the sensation that made the warning real: not a crash like a ship hitting a wall, but a prolonged, cold interruption, a shudder and scrape along the starboard side that many would later describe as strangely muted.

On the bridge, those six seconds registered as vibration and resistance—an event you could feel more than hear.

Captain Edward Smith was summoned to the bridge and arrived within minutes of the collision. Titanic did not shudder to an abrupt halt; instead, she eased down from her great speed into a gradual, uneasy quiet. The bridge's first task was not evacuation but understanding: What had they hit? How large was the damage? Was the ship still seaworthy?

The officers moved quickly through the chain of assessment—sending word to the lower decks, waiting for reports from the engineers and firemen, watching the ship's trim and her slowing headway for clues. In these early moments, no one on the bridge was yet contemplating lifeboats. They were trying to grasp the size of the wound and whether the ship could survive it.

Frederick Barrett and the firemen working in Boiler Room No. 6 understood the severity of the damage almost immediately. The impact tore open the ship's starboard side, and seawater poured in with force, flooding the space within moments. Frederick forced his way through the watertight door into Boiler Room No. 5, but an order came quickly: he was to return.

Illustration, Titanic Striking the Iceberg

By the time he did, water was already rising rapidly—eight feet deep in Boiler Room No. 6. The engineers moved to the pumps, attempting to slow the inevitable. At the same time, alarms carried through the machinery spaces. Orders followed in quick succession. The engine room signaled for stokers to abandon their posts and make for the deck.

Frederick began to withdraw again, but was stopped once more—this time ordered to remain in Boiler Room No. 5. Even there, the sea was not far behind. Water was already forcing its way in, spreading through the compartments faster than the men below could contain it.

As the water rose quickly in the boiler rooms, Chief Engineer Joseph Bell was already moving toward the bridge when he met Bruce Ismay at the top of the B Deck staircase. Ismay asked him directly whether he believed the ship had been seriously damaged. Bell did not minimize the situation. He told Ismay the damage was severe but added that he hoped the pumps might keep the flooding under control.[7]

There was nothing more to say.

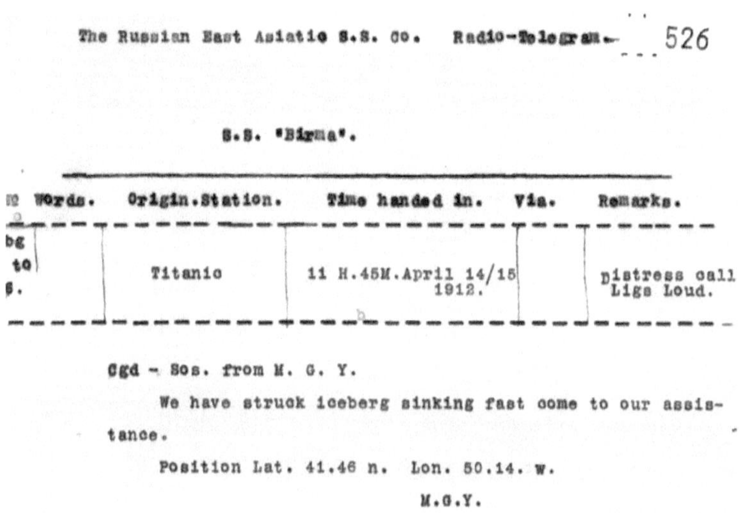

Titanic's Wireless Message, 11:45 P.M.

Ismay turned and returned to his cabin, while Bell continued on toward the bridge. The exchange was brief, factual, and unfinished—an assessment offered in motion, before the scale of the injury had fully declared itself.

By 11:45 p.m. on April 14, the uncertainty on the bridge had hardened into the recognition that Titanic was in grave trouble. Only then did the wireless operators receive the order that had not come in the first minutes after the collision: send a distress call.

The message went out with the ship's call sign, M.G.Y., crackling across the North Atlantic. It immediately reached the Russian steamer Birma, whose operator recorded it in the stark language of emergency:
"We have struck iceberg sinking fast come to our assistance. Position Lat. 41.46 N, Lon. 50.14 W."

The note was brief, the urgency unmistakable. The operator on Birma marked it plainly as a distress call—adding the remark "signals loud," evidence that Titanic's powerful transmitter still carried her voice clearly across the dark sea.

Inside the wireless room, operator Jack Phillips continued to send the signal repeatedly, alternating between the traditional distress code CQD and the newer SOS, hoping to reach every ship within range. This was the moment when routine communication gave way to crisis.

In those first critical minutes after the collision, the ship remained strangely quiet. No alarms rang through the decks, no public announcements echoed down the corridors, and no stewards were dispatched to wake sleeping passengers. There was no movement toward the lifeboats, no note of urgency in the public spaces.

On the decks above, passengers remained calm. Yet something was noticeably different. For many, the first sign that something was wrong was not the impact—it was the silence that followed. Titanic's engines, so steady and constant since leaving Queenstown, had gone silent. For travelers accustomed to the low, reassuring vibration of the ship beneath their feet, the sudden stillness felt unnatural. People stepped into the corridors, exchanged puzzled glances, and drifted toward the public rooms to ask the same hesitant question: Why have we stopped?

A small cluster of first-class passengers gathered in the lounge, where stewards—working hard to keep the atmosphere calm—offered brandy and coffee. The ship still sat level, the lights were bright, and there was no sense of panic. To steady nerves, the band was summoned to play a few light pieces. The music was gentle, almost cheerful, and for a moment the room took on the mood of a late, unplanned social hour.

But below, the truth was spreading much faster than reassurance could. Water had already begun to pour into the forward mailroom. Bags and sealed pouches floated as the clerks—realizing the severity of the flooding—worked frantically to save what they could. By midnight, the mailroom was fully flooded.[8]

And the water was moving aft.

By 12:30 a.m., the squash court one deck below was reported to be ten feet underwater, a depth that no message, no music, no warm drink could soften. On the surface, Titanic still looked steady. But the silence that had first unsettled the passengers was only the beginning. Titanic was sinking, and sinking fast.

The carpenter began sounding the ship, measuring the rate of flooding. Reports from the forward compartments grew steadily worse. One by one, the limits of the ship's design were being reached—and exceeded.

Above, officers calculated. Below, men fought the water. And between those two realities, thousands of passengers slept through the most critical minutes of the night. By then, the ship's fate was already sealed.

———————————❖———————————

The Stewardesses

Maude Slocombe was already in bed when the collision came—a muted, unmistakable thud that vibrated through the steelwork of the ship. It was not violent, not the kind of jolt that sent furniture sliding or passengers crying out, but she was experienced enough to know it was wrong. She rose quickly, pulled on a wrap, and stepped into the passageway.

There she encountered Second-in-Command Steward George Charles Dodd, moving briskly through the corridor. He told her, with the brisk efficiency of a man following orders, to get dressed and go up on deck. When Maude pressed him, quietly but firmly, for an explanation, he could offer none. He did not know what had happened. Only that she must go up.

When she reached the upper decks, Maude found a scene that surprised her. The air was cold, but the atmosphere among passengers remained almost cheerful. People chatted in small groups, commenting on the stillness of the engines or the unusual lateness of the hour. Some wrapped in coats, others still in evening clothes, they lingered under the bright electric lamps without alarm. Maude later spoke of this moment with admiration—the steadiness of the crew, the calm they projected, the way they guided passengers without revealing the worry growing below.

For a brief moment, Maude considered returning to her cabin to collect a few personal belongings. But when she descended partway down the stairwell, she met a sight that stopped her: water rising in the lower passageway, advancing with a quiet but steady certainty. It was enough to tell her that the situation was far more serious than anyone on deck yet understood. She turned back immediately, climbing toward the open air and the relative safety of the upper decks.

Behind her, the water continued its silent climb through the ship she had served only days before.

Mary Jane Sloan

The corridor outside the first-class cabins was quieter after eleven. Electric light burned steadily along the paneled walls where carpets muted footsteps, and the Atlantic itself seemed to be obeyed.

Mary Jane Sloan had already completed her late rounds. Doors checked, and lamps dimmed where requested. One elderly passenger tucked in with an extra blanket because the April night carried a sharper edge than expected. She knew which cabins preferred tea in the morning and which preferred not to be disturbed before nine. Order had its own rhythm.

Then came the tremor.

Not a crash. Not a roar. A long, almost thoughtful shudder beneath the soles of her shoes. The vibration traveled up through the floorboards and into her calves. Enough to interrupt a sentence. Not enough to send china sliding. She paused. Listened.

In the first-class corridors, curiosity travels faster than fear. Doors opened a few inches. Questions were asked in controlled voices.

"What was that?"

"Have we stopped?"

Mary answered the way she had been trained to answer.

"It's nothing, madam. Only precaution. Please dress warmly."

She moved from door to door, repeating the instruction. Lifejackets were retrieved from shelves. Some women laughed at the awkward cork bulk beneath silk dressing gowns. One asked if she might leave her jewels in the cabin safe. Another insisted on bringing her dog. Mary did not speculate or improvise; she simply relayed.

Within minutes, an officer appeared, telling her that the mailbags were afloat—a quiet but devastating confirmation that water had reached the lower decks. He gathered Mary Jane and another stewardess into his room and offered them each a small glass of whiskey and water. Mary Jane managed a laugh and asked whether he truly thought they needed it. He told them they did.

The other stewardess began to cry. When he turned to Mary Jane and asked if she was afraid, she told him she was not. He answered with the praise of someone who knew her well—"spoken like a true Ulster girl"—before rushing off to check whether any passengers had been injured. Mary Jane helped him into his greatcoat as he left. She never saw him again.

Not long after, she encountered Dr. O'Loughlin in the passageway. She asked him to tell her the truth, however grim. "Child," he answered, "things are very bad."

Instructions traveled downward through the hierarchy. Women and children to the boat deck. Calmly. With coats. She knew the route by memory. She had walked it a dozen times in daylight. From this corridor to the staircase. Up one level. Then another. She could have climbed it blind. Mary Jane Sloan never panicked—in that corridor, beneath electric light and carved oak, she had kept her voice level. She had performed order even as order thinned. Later, in a letter written from another ship, she would try to describe the sequence—how it unfolded, how it did not feel catastrophic at first. But in that moment, she was not writing. She was working.

She made a final round of the cabins in her section, knocking at doors, making sure her passengers were awake and properly dressed, urging them to put on their lifebelts. As she moved along the corridor, she met Thomas Andrews, the ship's builder. The expression on his face told her more than words could have. He saw her knocking on doors and told her she was doing right—see that every passenger had a lifebelt, he said, and then get one for yourself and go up on deck.[9]

On the boat deck, the night was wider than it should have been. Bright stars, breath turning white and officers moving with deliberate speed. Lifeboats uncovered, swung outward. Mary stepped back once her group was assembled. A stewardess does not claim space in the boat until instructed. Her task was to steady others.

Below her, the ship was already taking in water. At one point, she slipped away from the crowd, thinking she might return briefly to her cabin to retrieve a few pieces of jewelry. There had been time earlier in the evening when the danger still seemed distant. But by then the rhythm of the ship had changed. There was no time left. She returned to the deck instead.

One of the small bellboys recognized her immediately. He pointed toward a lifeboat already crowded with women and said, "Miss Sloan, that's your boat—Number 12."

Mary Jane hesitated. "Child," she replied, "how do you know? I will wait for another."

The boat pushed off without her.

She remained standing on the deck a while longer, watching the officers, listening to the steady firing of the distress rockets overhead. Most passengers still did not grasp what was happening, but she was close enough to see something change in Captain Edward Smith. The composure that had held the night together was beginning to crack.

"I saw Captain Smith getting excited," she later recalled. "Passengers would not have noticed, but I did. I knew then we were soon going."

The rockets were rising into the sky one after another now. Mary Jane decided that if anyone asked her again to take a seat in a lifeboat, she would not refuse.

First Class: Helen Candee

Helen Candee was preparing for a bath when the ship struck the iceberg—"like striking the top of a mountain under the sea," she would later write. There was no dramatic crash, just a deep, unnatural shock that moved through the steel beneath her feet. Curious and uneasy, she stepped into the corridor and stopped a steward to ask what had happened. He urged her not to alarm anyone, assuring her that nothing was amiss and advising her to return to her cabin. She did not. Years of hardship and responsibility had sharpened her instincts, and nothing about the ship's sudden stillness felt ordinary.

Before she had time to gather her thoughts, Hugh Woolner was at her side. "Woolner laid an arm over my shoulder," she recalled. "The gesture gave me an unwarranted sense of security."

Together, they returned to her stateroom so she could collect a few essentials. The corridors were beginning to fill, passengers and crew moving with the uncertain urgency of people who sense that something is wrong but have not yet been told how wrong. As they made their way upward, they encountered Edward Kent, the American architect she had become acquainted with during the voyage. His eyes fell immediately on the small bag in Helen's hand. She remembered his firm objection—"You can't take baggage with you!" Knowing she might not keep her belongings with her, and sensing the seriousness of the situation, Helen entrusted Edward with two small objects of great personal value: a silver flask and a small ivory cameo of her mother. It was a gesture made in haste, grounded in trust. The item would later be recovered with Kent's body and returned to her in New York.

Helen Candee's Cameo

They made their way upward, toward the higher decks where passengers were gathering.

As they approached the upper decks, a group of stokers suddenly emerged from below—men fleeing the rising water that was already sweeping through the lowest compartments. Helen never forgot the look on their faces. "Each face reflected the sight he had seen, the sight of coming death," she wrote later. These were the men who had seen the damage firsthand, who understood with terrible clarity what the passengers around them did not yet grasp.

Then, in a moment as abrupt as it was haunting, their junior officer gave a short, sharp command: Halt.

The men stopped. No protest, no hesitation. At his order, they turned back toward the flooding decks they had just escaped. One by one, they descended—back into the heat, the steam, and the seawater rushing through the ship's torn steel.

Helen watched them go with a shock that settled into reverence. "I looked with profound admiration at the descending column of men, who could courageously relinquish their life," she wrote. It was, to her, one of the most heroic moments of the night: ordinary seamen obeying duty over fear, returning to a place from which they knew they would not return.

Their silent descent, disappearing into the ship's wounded core, stayed with her for the rest of her life.

Helen continued upward toward the lifeboats, the truth of the disaster settling around her with every step she took into the cold night. When Helen and Woolner reached the

Boat Deck, the scene was not one of calm. Distress rockets were bursting over the ship—white arcs falling into the cold dark—and the captain was ordering the lifeboats swung out from their davits. The deck had become a place of brisk, controlled activity, officers calling instructions, stewards gathering women and children, passengers clustering at the rails in the freezing air.

As the lifeboats were lowered one by one, Helen and Woolner stood for a time together, watching the sky. The brightness of the stars was what she remembered most— how clear and sharp they seemed above the growing urgency below, how vast the night looked over the ship that was slowly settling into it.

Those quiet moments, under a sky impossibly bright, would be her last on Titanic's deck.

First Class: Edith Rosenbaum

Edith Rosenbaum felt the impact as a slight bump—enough to draw her attention, but not enough to cause significant alarm. Curious, she stepped out of her cabin and made her way toward the deck, catching sight of the iceberg sliding past the ship like a pale wall in the darkness. Before doing so, she later claimed, she paused to lock each of her trunks—packed with valuable Paris couture she was transporting for the spring season—an instinctive act for a woman who had spent her life moving garments, samples, and merchandise across continents.

She arrived in the first-class lounge, watching the early stirrings of evacuation with a mixture of curiosity and confusion. When she saw her room steward, Robert

Wareham, she called him over, anxious not about herself but about her luggage. Rumors were circulating that Titanic had been damaged but would be towed to Halifax while passengers were transferred to another ship. Edith feared her trunks—her livelihood—might be lost in the transfer. She handed Wareham her trunk keys, asking if he could see them safely through Customs.

He gave her a blunt reply: "Kiss your trunks good-bye."

It was not the reassurance she hoped for, but Wareham did one thing for her before returning to his duties below. He went back to her cabin and fetched the small object she prized above everything else: her papier-mâché pig, a music-box "mascot" covered in black-and-white spotted fur that played The Maxixe when its tail was wound. Her mother had given it to her the year before, after Edith survived a serious car accident in France—where pigs were believed to bring good luck. Edith had promised she would never travel without it.

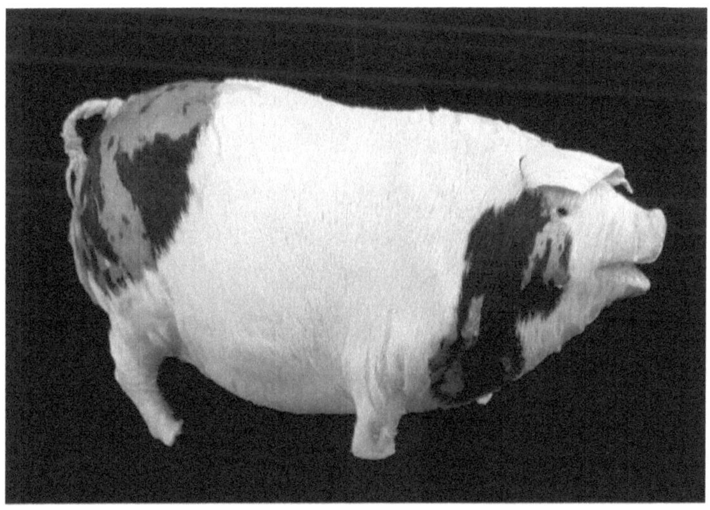

Ediths Music Box Pig

Wareham returned with the toy wrapped carefully in a blanket, pressing it into her hands. With that small comfort tucked securely under her arm, Edith made her way toward the Boat Deck, eventually reaching the starboard side where the night had taken on a sharper urgency—officers calling orders, rockets rising into the sky, lifeboats being uncovered and swung out.

There she caught the attention of J. Bruce Ismay, chairman of the White Star Line, who recognized her and took note that she had not yet boarded a lifeboat. He admonished her for lingering and directed her firmly toward a stairway leading to the deck below, where one of the starboard boats was being loaded.

Clutching her small pig, she obeyed, stepping into the heart of the evacuation that would carry her away from the great ship she had admired only days before.

Second Class, Elizabeth and Violet Mellenger

For Elizabeth Mellenger and her teenage daughter Violet, the first sign that something was wrong came not from a jolt—they felt little of that in second class—but from the strange quiet that settled over their deck. Then came the distant hum of footsteps, doors opening, voices rising in the corridor. Like many in second class, Elizabeth stepped out to ask a steward what had happened. The reassurance she received was typical of those early minutes: nothing to worry about, just a precaution.

But soon passengers began drifting toward the stairwells, some carrying overcoats, others clutching children by the hand. Word spread unevenly—passed from cabin to cabin, repeated in half-thought whispers—that everyone was being asked to go up on deck. The ship, people said, had struck ice. Better to dress warmly. Better to bring your lifebelt.

Recreation, Titanic Passageway

Elizabeth, realizing the seriousness behind the calm faces, roused Violet and made sure she put on warm clothes beneath her coat. Lifebelts were retrieved from their hooks. The two joined the gathering line of second-class families moving upward through narrow stairways, held back at times by stewards controlling access to the first-class decks above. This was one of the known frustrations of second-class evacuation that night—delays not born of neglect, but of long corridors, locked gates, and the need for crew oversight at every transition between classes.

Eventually, a steward opened the barrier, guiding groups upward in small clusters. Elizabeth kept Violet close, her hand firm on her daughter's shoulder as they joined the flow of passengers emerging into the cold night air. On the open deck, the scene was both orderly and shocking: crew calling for women and children, lifeboats being launched, the faint smell of cordite still lingering from the distress rockets that had already burst into the sky.

There was confusion, as there was everywhere. Many passengers hesitated, believing the ship too solid, too immense to be in real danger. Others worried about leaving husbands or sons. The pattern of that night is clear: second-class women and children were directed firmly toward the boats once they reached the open deck, their presence noted, their names checked off by stewards working to maintain order.

Elizabeth and Violet would have stood among the cluster of second-class families waiting their turn—cold air stinging their faces, the glow of electric lights reflecting off polished white paint, the sea stretching black and still beyond the rail. Officers were calling for women and children. Some boats were launching only half-full; others were filling steadily. The ship still looked level, deceptively stable, even as water crept farther into its hull.

A steward finally ushered them toward one of the boats. Violet was lifted to the gunwale, her mother behind her. Second-class women were encouraged forward with increasing urgency as the night deepened.

Elizabeth would have felt the decision tighten around her: the need to climb into a small wooden boat in the freezing dark, trusting the crew, trusting the ropes, trusting anything that wasn't the sinking ship behind her. She took Violet's hand and stepped in.

Second Class: Brown Family

On the night of April 14, the Brown family retired early. Edith remembered drifting into sleep, the steady hum of the engines lulling her as it had every night of the voyage. She awoke to a distant sound muffled by steel, and a slight, unsettling jar that ran through the ship. "A violent shiver," she later called it. Startled, she roused her mother, who in turn called for her father to investigate.

He went up on deck to see what had happened and soon returned, calm enough to reassure them. The ship, he said, had struck an iceberg, but there was no danger. His composed manner, along with the ship's steady, level feel beneath their feet, was convincing enough. Edith and her mother lay back down, trusting the confidence of a man who had crossed oceans before.

Only a few minutes passed before he returned again. This time his expression was different—ashen, strained, the face of someone trying not to alarm the people he loved. He told them quietly but firmly to get up and get dressed. There was, he admitted, "some concern over the ship's safety."

The tone of the night had changed. What had been a strange interruption was becoming something else—a slow, dawning understanding that the great ship was in real trouble.

"We dressed hurriedly," Edith remembered, "and I put on extra warm garments." Her father returned to their cabin carrying lifebelts—one for her mother, one for Edith, and finally one for himself. He fastened them carefully, the quiet efficiency of the act doing little to mask the worry now clear on his face.

Together they climbed toward the boat deck, joining the growing stream of second-class families moving upward through narrow stairwells and dimly lit corridors. When they reached the open air, Edith saw that the evacuation was already underway. People were filing into lifeboats with a mixture of reluctance and confusion, the ship still lying so steady that danger seemed almost impossible. In later years Edith would recall her father pointing out a distant light—"that little blighter," he said, convinced it belonged to a ship coming to their rescue.

But around them, the mood was tightening. Edith recalled disorder growing as space in the final boats dwindled. Men tried to climb in; an officer fired his revolver into the air, shouting that he would shoot anyone who jumped. She believed this was the kernel of later stories claiming officers had killed passengers. One man did leap into their lifeboat, No. 14, as it was being lowered—a foreigner, she said, whose nationality she could not determine. "It was too late to make him get back." Except for him, the officer, and the four firemen assigned to row, she remembered the boat as almost entirely women and children. It was launched at 1:30 a.m.

Titanic's portside Second-Class boat deck, with Lifeboat No. 14 being seen as the second Lifeboat from the left.

Even then, as the hour grew later, many aboard still believed Titanic could not sink. Edith wrote that it seemed "almost impossible" for something so vast and luxurious to be lost to the sea. But once their lifeboat reached the water and began pulling away, the truth became undeniable. They watched the ship in silence. "As our lifeboat was lowered," she said, "the band was playing a hymn."

Third Class: Leah Aks

Leah was jolted awake not by the collision but by a knock on her cabin door. The corridor outside was already alive with noise—shouts, hurried footsteps, fragments of instructions she could not fully understand. She hurriedly dressed her 10-month-old son, Filly, and followed the flow of third-class passengers toward the aft stairway, the only route many of them were being allowed to use. At the bottom of that narrow staircase, Leah joined a growing crowd of women and children waiting for word from the crew.

Realizing she hadn't retrieved life jackets, she returned to her cabin long enough to find them, slipping one over herself and wrapping another awkwardly around Filly. Returning to the deck, she found the route upward blocked—too many people pressing toward a locked gate, too few crew to manage the crush. Trapped at the bottom of the third-class staircase, she and Filly waited with other women while stewards tried to organize a way forward.

Around 12:30 a.m., stewards finally opened the gate and allowed the group of third-class women and children to move upward. The stairs were crowded, nearly impassable for a woman carrying a baby. Men on the deck above saw the women and infants stranded below and began to improvise a solution. One by one, they formed a human ladder, reaching down to hoist women up through the railings when the stairs became impassable. Leah felt herself lifted, pulled upward toward the first-class boat deck, still clutching Filly tightly.

Suddenly on deck, they were met with bright lights, finer railings, stewards in uniform—an enormous contrast to the cramped decks below. By now, there were panicked voices and the sharp crack of distress rockets lighting the sky. Lifeboats were already being lowered. The air was cold and frantic.

Filly's clothing had been rushed, and seeing him uncovered, a first-class passenger—Madeline Astor, herself young and newly pregnant—stepped forward and gently laid her silk scarf over the baby's head. It was one of the rare, small mercies of the night.[10]

But the chaos around them was growing sharper.
According to one later account preserved by Leah's family,
a distraught man—recently turned away from a lifeboat—
rushed toward her shouting, "I'll show you women and
children first!" Exactly what happened next differs across
survivor recollections, but all agree on the essential
tragedy: Leah and her infant son became separated in the
confusion.

Illustration, Lifeboats being Lowered on Titanic

Some versions say the baby was torn from her arms as she was carried up the stairs. Others say that a man grabbed the child and threw him into a lifeboat already being lowered. Still others simply record that mother and son were pushed apart in the crush of passengers on the starboard side.

What is certain is that Leah found herself suddenly alone. She searched frantically along the deck, asking after the baby, peering into the faces of other passengers. Before she could locate her child, someone urged — or pushed — her toward a waiting lifeboat. Numb and stunned, Leah was placed into Lifeboat No. 13, one of the final boats leaving the starboard side. As it dropped toward the black water, she became one of the few third-class women to reach a lifeboat that night — but she believed her infant had been lost. It was 1:40 a.m.

Third Class: Rhoda Abbott

Rhoda Abbott and her two teenage sons were asleep in their third-class cabin when Titanic struck the iceberg. The impact was slight, but within minutes, around 12:15 a.m., a steward was knocking at doors, urging families to put on lifejackets and make their way to the deck. Rhoda roused Eugene and Rossmore, helping them dress quickly in the cramped quarters before joining the stream of third-class passengers funneling through the narrow corridors.

Progress upward was slow. Third-class families waited in tight, anxious lines behind other passengers, following stewards who guided them through the few unlocked routes toward the upper decks. Rhoda kept her sons close as they climbed stairways crowded with families speaking in dozens of languages, all trying to understand what was happening and where they were meant to go.

Eventually, they reached the second-class saloon area, where many third-class passengers were being held until officers could manage the flow onto the boat deck. There, amid the confusion and rising fear, Rossmore—just thirteen—knelt to pray, asking that his mother be spared even if he and his brother were not. Rhoda gathered them close, refusing to let them out of her sight.

Though the rule of the night was "women and children first," Rhoda's sons—aged 13 and 16—were young enough to accompany her through the crowd. Together they made their way toward the starboard side, where officers were loading the final boats. By the time they arrived, Collapsible C was already being prepared—one of the last chances for survival as the ship's bow was noticeably lower in the water.

When Rhoda reached the edge of the lifeboat, officers indicated that she, as a woman, could board. But her sons, considered too old to qualify as "children," would be held back. Faced with the possibility of leaving them behind, Rhoda stepped back. She refused to take a place that her boys could not follow her. As another survivor later recalled, "She told me she would have gotten into the lifeboat if there hadn't been so many people around. So she and her sons kept together."

It was an act of instinctive loyalty, a mother's refusal to be separated from her children in the darkest moment of their lives. Rhoda and her sons remained on deck together as Collapsible C was lowered away into the freezing night. What followed for them—minutes, perhaps—was part of the ship's final, tragic descent.

[1] British Wreck Commissioner's Inquiry, Report of a Formal Investigation into the Loss of the S.S. "Titanic", evidence of Frederick Barrett, fireman, day 18, questions 13,590–13,600 (London: HMSO, 1912).

[2] "Titanic History, Facts and Stories". Titanic Museum Belfast. Archived from the original on 6 January 2021

[3] Mowbray, Jay Henry (1912a). The sinking of the Titanic.

[4] Hsu, Jeremy (17 April 2012). "How Marconi's Wireless Tech Helped Save Titanic Passengers". msnbc.com. Archived from the original on 6 January 2021.

[5] https://en.wikipedia.org/wiki/Sinking_of_the_Titanic

[6] Winocour, Jack (1960). The Story of the Titanic As Told by Its Survivors. Dover Publications. pp. 253, 254

[7] Hodgson, Barrie B.; Freer, Ann (2013). Tarn to Titanic: Life and Times of Joseph Bell Chief Engineer (1st ed.). Clearline Assistance UK Ltd.

[8] McCluskie, Tom (1998). Anatomy of the Titanic.

[9] Mary Sloan," Encyclopedia Titanica.

[10] Julie Gruenbaum Fax, "Titanic Survivor's Son Recounts Mother's Story," Jewish Journal, April 10, 2012.

Chapter 6 — Launching the Lifeboats

She gave a long, slow, steady dive and we knew she was going.

— The Loss of the S.S. Titanic, 1912

THE OFFICIAL EVACUATION HAD begun just after midnight.

At 12:05 a.m.. twenty-five minutes after striking the iceberg, Captain Edward Smith gave the order to uncover the lifeboats, muster the passengers, and prepare them for an emergency. Passengers were waking in their cabins, puzzled by the sudden silence: the steady throb of the engines and the faint vibration through the decks had stopped, leaving an uneasy stillness in their place.

Smith also ordered that distress calls be sent at once. In the wireless room, Jack Phillips and Harold Bride took down the position calculated by Fourth Officer Joseph Boxhall and began tapping out distress signals into the night. Boxhall's estimate, hurriedly made in the confusion, placed Titanic on the west side of the ice belt and was off by about 13.5 nautical miles.[1]

There was no loudspeaker system or general alarm aboard Titanic. What there was, was men and women with voices and shoes on carpet, moving from door to door through the long passageways, knocking, calling, pushing into dark cabins to shake awake whoever was sleeping inside. The message was the same each time: dress warmly, put on your lifebelt, get up to the boat deck.

The ship was sinking the same for everyone. The information was not.

In first class, stewards were responsible for only a handful of cabins each. They had time — time to help passengers into their coats, to fasten a lifejacket, to walk someone personally up to the deck. It was orderly, even courteous. In second and third class, one steward might be responsible for dozens of passengers spread across a maze of corridors. There was no time for courtesy. Doors came open, lights snapped on, and the instruction was brief and already moving down the hall: lifebelts on, go up top.

In third class, especially, families and single travelers were often left to find their own way after being told to come on deck. Many passengers and even some crew members hesitated. Some refused to believe anything serious was wrong with such a grand, "unsinkable" ship; others did not want to leave the warmth and bright lights inside for the freezing, black air outside.

On the forward well deck, where chunks of ice lay scattered from the impact, some younger passengers kicked and tossed the broken pieces around, turning them into makeshift footballs. For a few surreal minutes, it felt like a strange midnight game rather than the beginning of a disaster.

Up on the boat deck, officers and crew were wrestling with the practical problem of saving lives. Titanic carried only 20 lifeboats: 16 wooden boats slung on davits along the sides of the ship—eight on each side—and four collapsible boats with wooden bottoms and canvas sides. On paper, the lifeboats could each carry up to 68 people.

Altogether, if every seat were filled, they could hold 1,178 souls. It sounded like a large number until set beside the reality: more than 2,200 people were on board.

Even if everything went perfectly, there was room for barely half of those now being shaken awake in the quiet, slanting corridors of the great liner. Additionally, the collapsibles were stored upside down, with their sides folded in, and had to be set up correctly before being dragged to the davits for lowering. Two were tucked under the wooden lifeboats, and the other two were lashed on top of the officers' quarters, high and nearly out of reach. Each of those heavy craft weighed several tons and would have to be manhandled down to the boat deck, costing precious time.

By midnight, the collision had become a flooding problem measured in compartments and minutes. The question was no longer whether the ship would go down, but how much time remained before the machinery spaces went with it. Chief Engineer Joseph Bell and his men kept working anyway — maintaining steam where they could, running the pumps, holding onto the lights.

Later accounts have Bell saying, after he understood that the water was beating the barriers and moving aft: "My God, we're doomed." Whether those were his exact words is hard to say. What is not hard to say is what he knew in that moment, and what his men knew. The flooding would not be stopped. The ship's own design, the compartments that were supposed to save her, had already done the math.

They stayed at their posts, regardless. The engineering staff focused on keeping the ship operational as long as the machinery spaces remained workable: maintaining steam where possible, keeping pumps running, and preserving electrical power and lighting as long as the ship's internal layout allowed.

There is a version of the Titanic story that has become almost fixed in public memory: the band on deck, the music holding steady as the night worsens; the lights still burning in windows as the ship angles downward. Whether true or partly constructed after the fact, music on deck required a deck that could still function. Lifeboats could be lowered only in the dark if crews could still see what they were doing. The lights did not stay on by sentiment. They stayed on because men in the engine and boiler rooms kept them on—feeding boilers, maintaining steam, and holding the electrical plant as long as the sea allowed.

Whatever one believes about the band's final minutes, the broader truth is more complicated and less cinematic: Titanic remained operational longer than it had any right to, and that bought time—real minutes—for people to find their way upward and for boats to be lowered.

But Joseph and most of the engineers remained below, never abandoning their posts and working until the end. However, later testimony recounted that at least some engineering personnel were eventually released to go on deck, but by then, nearing 2 a.m., the lifeboats were gone. A small group of engineers was last seen on the starboard side near the electric crane, standing together on the boat deck.

Joseph Bell was last seen also around 2:00 a.m. attempting to reach the bridge by telephone—seeking confirmation, instruction, or simply an updated picture of what the ship was doing above. No reply came. By then, the ship's fate was no longer a question of engineering. It was a question of time.

And in those final minutes, time belonged to the sea.

❖

12:45 am to 2:05 a.m.

From 12:55 to 1:10 a.m., four lifeboats—Nos. 1, 3, 6, and 8—were launched carrying only first-class passengers and crew. Lifeboat 1 left with 12 occupants, Lifeboat 3 with 35, Lifeboat 6 with 24, and Lifeboat 8 with about 30 people. It was not until 1:20 a.m. that Lifeboat 9, the first to carry third-class passengers, was lowered away.

Lifeboat No. 6, 12:55 a.m.

Lifeboat No. 6 hung on the port side of the Titanic, one of fourteen clinker-built wooden boats designed to carry 65 people. When it was lowered at 12:55 a.m., scarcely more than two dozen were aboard—far fewer than the boat could hold, and far fewer than the night would demand.

Helen Candee reached Lifeboat 6 amid the rising urgency on the port side. Officers were calling for women and children; stewards guided passengers forward; the ship's slight list and the bitter wind made every movement feel sharper. As Helen stepped into the lifeboat, she slipped—perhaps from the awkward angle of the hull, perhaps from the rush of bodies pressing in—and fell hard enough to fracture her ankle. She said nothing at the time, only steadied herself and settled into the narrow wooden seat as the boat jerked away from the davits.

Also in Lifeboat 6 was another first-class woman traveling alone: Margaret Brown, later known to the world as "the Unsinkable Molly Brown." As Lifeboat 6 swung outward from the port side, the women inside realized with growing alarm that only two men—Quartermaster Robert Hichens at the tiller and lookout Frederick Fleet at an oar—had been assigned to the small, half-filled boat. Two members of the à la carte restaurant staff were also onboard: Ruth Bowker and Mabel Martin, the only two female cashiers on the ship.

The small lifeboat creaked uneasily as it descended. The wind was razor-cold, and below them the black Atlantic heaved under the gleam of Titanic's lights. The boat swung close to the Titanic's hull, scraping dangerously against it. Several women voiced their concern aloud—there were not enough men to manage the boat, not enough hands to row, and not enough strength to keep them clear of the sinking ship.

Their pleas rose upward to Second Officer Charles Lightoller, who stood at the davits above, supervising the lowering. He looked around for a crewman to send—but there were none within reach. With no sailors available and the lifeboat already dropping toward the sea, time was running out.

At that moment, Major Arthur Godfrey Peuchen, a wealthy Canadian and an experienced yachtsman, stepped forward and volunteered his help. Lightoller hesitated—his strict rule of "women and children only" had been unyielding all night. But the shortage of crew was undeniable. After a brief moments pause, he allowed Peuchen to board by sliding down the ropes into the lifeboat as it descended. He was the only adult male passenger Lightoller ever permitted into a lifeboat that night.

Cape worn by Helen Candee in the Lifeboat

Once Peuchen reached the thwarts, the dynamic shifted. Between him, Fleet, Hichens, and the women—many of whom, including Helen and Margaret, would soon take up oars—the boat gained the hands it needed to pull away from Titanic's towering hull.

Despite Helen's injured ankle, she took an oar, bracing herself against the pain. Together, the desperate survivors pulled the heavy, unwieldy boat away from the suction zone beside the sinking liner. Above them, the Titanic loomed impossibly large, her rows of lit portholes rising like windows in a cliff face. The oars were slippery. But the work was necessary, and Helen, like Margaret, did it without hesitation.

As Lifeboat 6 creaked its way further into the darkness, Helen looked back at the ship that had been a world of bright rooms and warm corridors only hours before. In the end, the little clinker-built boat—meant for sixty-five, carrying only around twenty-four—pulled away into the black water, with lives would be forever shaped by the hours that followed.

Below deck, things were looking dire. Two engineers, Herbert Harvey and Jonathan Shepherd, died in boiler room 5 when, at around 12:45, the bunker door separating it from the flooded No. 6 boiler room collapsed, and they were swept away by "a wave of green foam," according to leading fireman Frederick Barrett, who barely escaped.

Lifeboats were sent down from the davits every few minutes on both sides of the ship, yet many left with far fewer people than they could safely carry. Boat No. 5 pulled away with only 41 people aboard, No. 8 with 39. The evacuation itself was chaotic, and people were hurt as they tried to escape. One woman slipped into the gap between lifeboat No. 10 and the ship's side, only to be seized by the ankle and hauled back onto the promenade deck before managing to board on a second attempt. In another incident, first-class passenger Annie Stengel suffered several broken ribs when a German-American doctor and his brother leapt into Boat No. 5, landing on her and knocking her unconscious.

Once in the boats, the danger was not over. Boat No. 3 narrowly avoided catastrophe when one of the davits jammed during lowering, leaving the passengers briefly at risk of being thrown into the sea before the problem was cleared.

From 1:20 a.m. to 1:45, finding a lifeboat became increasingly urgent. The boat deck was now a crush of movement and noise.

The bow was settling lower, the list more pronounced, and officers were trying to impose order on something rapidly slipping beyond control. Lifeboat 9 went next, swinging out over the black water with a mix of women, children, and a handful of men from second and third class, along with crew at the oars. It left with just over forty people, though later survivors from other boats were transferred into it until more than seventy crowded its thwarts.

Nearby, Lifeboat 10 dropped away almost alongside, carrying around fifty-five passengers—mostly women and children from second and third class who had finally come up from the lower decks, herded by a few determined crew, including third-class steward John Edward Hart.[2]

Only minutes later, at about 1:25, the pace quickened. Boats 11 and 12 were loaded and lowered one after the other, officers shouting to hurry as the deck tilted and the emergency rockets burst overhead. Lifeboat 12 went down with just over forty people, many of them third-class women and children mixed with a few men and stewards. Lifeboat 11 was packed more tightly—around seventy souls—so full that people were pressed shoulder to shoulder on the wooden benches as she dropped toward the sea, the ship's massive hull towering beside them.

Lifeboat No. 12

Mary Jane "May" Sloan had been working long after most passengers had begun to feel the unease spreading through the ship. As a stewardess she belonged to the quiet machinery that kept order aboard Titanic, calming passengers, guiding women through corridors, and helping them into coats and lifebelts. Even as the cold crept deeper into the ship and the officers' voices grew sharper, she remained at her post, helping others toward the boats.

Lifeboat 12 waited along the port side. It had been lowered earlier than many of the others, likely the third boat launched from that side, at about 1:20 in the morning. The officers were still struggling to persuade women to enter the boats. The ship looked steady, its lights bright, its decks orderly enough that danger still felt theoretical.

Most of those stepping into Boat 12 were second-class women—passengers who had been brought up from the middle decks by stewards and stewardesses like Sloan. They crossed the narrow gap one by one while sailors steadied the boat below. Sloan entered with them, still thinking like a member of the crew, scanning faces, making sure no one slipped as they stepped down.

When the ropes released, the boat held only twenty-eight or thirty people. One young man jumped in as it began to lower, landing among the women and the two sailors assigned to the boat.

The descent was slow. The towering hull of Titanic slid upward beside them until the lifeboat reached the water and drifted free. For a time they rowed in uncertain silence, the ship still blazing with light behind them. Then, in the darkness of the Atlantic, the scattered boats began to gather.

Later, when the sharp blast of Second Officer Charles Lightoller's whistle carried across the water, the oarsmen of Boat 12 pulled hard toward the sound. Along with Lifeboat 4 they reached the overturned Collapsible B, where men clung to the upturned hull in the freezing Atlantic. About sixteen more survivors were hauled aboard.

Boat 12 eventually also came alongside Lifeboat 14 where Fifth Officer Harold Lowe was organizing a small fleet. Lowe began redistributing passengers, shifting people from one boat to another so that he could take a few emptier boats back toward the wreckage. Boat 12 received many of those transfers.

Ten or twelve survivors came from Boat 14. Two or three crewmen from Collapsible D climbed aboard as well. The small lifeboat that had left the ship with fewer than thirty people now carried more than forty.

The night was not finished with them yet.

Lifeboat No. 14

The air smelled sharp—salt and iron and something colder rising from the dark water below. Lifeboat 14 hung beside the deck like an open doorway into the night.

The lifeboat was already filling—faces pale in the electric light, strangers pressed shoulder to shoulder. A few men stood at the oars, waiting for the signal. Above them the towering hull of Titanic rose like a wall of glowing windows. Near the davits where Lifeboat 14 waited, families were being separated in the practiced order the officers insisted upon: women and children first.

Edith Brown clutched her mother's hand as her father helped them toward the boat. He moved with the steady calm of someone determined not to frighten a child. One by one he guided them across. Then he stepped back.

Edith would remember the moment with painful clarity for the rest of her life. Her father stood there on the deck beside the rail, his back turned toward the boat as it prepared to lower. In later recollections she remembered him standing quietly, a cigar between his fingers after he had seen his wife and daughter safely aboard.

"My father helped us into boat number 14 and then turned away," she later wrote. "That was the last I ever saw of him. I saw him standing there with his back toward us. He never turned round while we could see him."

Elizabeth and Edith Brown, along with Elizabeth and Violet Mellinger, were all aboard when, at about 1:30 in the morning, the ropes were released, close to capacity with about sixty passengers and crew. The scene around it was fraying at the edges now: some men tried to push forward, others hung back in disbelief.

As Lifeboat 14 began its slow descent, creaking downward along the side of the great ship, Elizabeth looked up, searching the deck where they had just stood. The people there seemed distant already, silhouettes leaning over the rail, watching the boats disappear into the dark. When the lifeboat touched the water, the sea felt enormous.

Oars dipped into the freezing Atlantic. The lifeboat drifted into the darkness while the lights of Titanic still burned behind them, steady and bright, as if the night itself had not yet decided what would happen next.

By 1:35, two more boats—16 and 15—were being worked at the davits almost at once. Lifeboat 16 went down with roughly fifty-six aboard, a heavy mix of second and third-class women and children, and a thin scattering of crew to row. Lifeboat 15 was one of the most crowded to leave, crammed with around seventy-one people as it dropped—women and children jammed together, with just enough seamen to handle the oars. It rode perilously low in the water, so overladen that any sudden movement might have swamped them.

At about 1:40, Collapsible C was brought to the davits and hastily filled with forty-seven people—mostly first-class women and children, a few men, and crew—its canvas sides hurriedly raised as it was lowered away. The air was full of shouted orders, crying children, and the relentless hiss and boom of vented steam.

Lifeboat No. 11

On the starboard side, Lifeboat 11 launched at 1:37 a.m. It was first brought level with A Deck so that stewards could guide women and children over the railing and into the crowded space below. Steward Wheelton later reported escorting roughly forty women through the corridor and down onto the deck where the boat waited, its thwarts already filling with passengers from both first and second class.

In that shuffle of people, Edith Rosenbaum stepped forward holding her small, fur-covered papier-mâché pig. A crewman, perhaps mistaking it for a baby in the dim light, snatched it from her hands and tossed it into the lifeboat ahead of her. A male passenger then helped Edith over the rail and down into the boat as more women and children were being urged forward.

Mothers with infants, second-class families, stewardesses including Maude Slocombe and a handful of men allowed to assist the crew all pressed toward the thinning space. Lifeboat 11 was one of the most heavily loaded boats that left the Titanic. Contemporary estimates range from 68 to more than 70 people, including nearly a dozen children, around thirty women, several stewardesses, three male passengers, and more than a dozen members of the crew. The lowering was uneven, at times jerking dangerously against the davits. At the last moment a baby was thrown into the boat by someone on the deck above.

The boat, crammed far beyond comfort, began to pull away from the Titanic. Edith soon realized she was surrounded by frightened children—crying, fidgeting, clinging to their mothers or to one another. She reached for the small pig the crewman had tossed in before her. Winding its tail, she let the toy play its jaunty tune, The Maxixe. The bright, tinkling music seemed out of place against the cold black sea, yet it soothed the children, capturing their attention and easing their fear.

Among them, nestled somewhere in the lifeboat's crowded interior, was ten-month-old Frank "Filly" Aks, separated from his mother in the rush of commotion moments before. Many years later, Edith would meet him again—as an adult—and show him the very same little music-box pig that had once played for him in the frozen Atlantic night.

As Lifeboat 11 drifted farther from the sinking ship, its passengers watched the lights of the Titanic rise and fall against the dark horizon. Edith, clutching her unlikely mascot, focused instead on the children beside her— keeping them calm with a tune meant for another world entirely.

By 1:45 a.m., Lifeboat 2, one of the small emergency cutters, was being lowered under Fourth Officer Boxhall's charge. It left with barely two dozen aboard, about twenty-five or twenty-six people in a boat built for more. As it pulled away into the darkness, the great ship's bow was far lower than it had been only twenty-five minutes earlier. In that short span, a rush of boats had gone down from both sides—some under-filled, some dangerously crowded—while hundreds of passengers still milled on the slanting decks, only beginning to understand that the lifeboats were running out and time was almost gone.

Lifeboat No. 13

At 1:40 a.m. there were only two lifeboats remaining. Lifeboat No. 13 was overcrowded—nearly seventy people aboard, far exceeding the anticipated capacity. Sitting among them was Leah Aks, a despondent mother who had been separated from her infant son.

As they were being lowered from the starboard side, another lifeboat, Lifeboat 15, descended above them. For a moment, it seemed as if it would come down directly on top of them. Only at the last instant was the descent halted, checked just in time to prevent the two boats from colliding.

Lifeboat 13 then pulled away.[3] It was 1:43 a.m.

The last boat to be launched was collapsible D, which left at 02:05 with 25 people aboard. As it was being lowered, two more men jumped into the boat. By now, the water had reached the boat deck, and the forecastle was deep underwater.

On the lower decks, the scene was unfolding differently. Leading Fireman Charles Hendrickson later recalled looking down the third-class corridors and seeing groups of steerage passengers clustered with their trunks and bundles, standing as if waiting for orders that would never come. This learned, stoic passivity was shaped by generations of being told to obey social superiors rather than to act on their own.

One of the surviving third-class men, August Wennerström, recalled the same scene in the dining saloon: hundreds of third-class passengers gathered in a great circle around a preacher, praying, crying, and begging God and Mary for help, yet making no move to escape. "They lay there and yelled," he wrote, "never lifting a hand to help themselves," as if their will had drained away and they were waiting for heaven to decide their fate.

SS Californian

Earlier that night, the steamer SS Californian had sent Titanic a warning about heavy ice ahead. Captain Stanley Lord, wary of driving his slower ship into the vast field of drift ice, ordered Californian to stop at about 10:00 p.m. and wait for daylight before attempting to work through it.

By 11:30 p.m.—just ten minutes before Titanic struck the iceberg—Californian's only wireless operator, Cyril Evans, switched off his set for the night and went to bed. Out on the bridge, Third Officer Charles Groves noticed a large ship to starboard, some 10 to 12 miles away, which he said turned sharply to port and then appeared to stop. Later reviewers of the disaster would argue that if Evans had remained at his post even fifteen minutes longer, he might have heard Titanic's distress calls and helped save hundreds of lives.

A little over an hour after Evans retired, Second Officer Herbert Stone watched five white rockets burst over the still, motionless ship. Unsure what the signals meant, he reported them to Captain Lord in the chartroom, but no orders were given to proceed through the ice or close the distance. Stone, increasingly uneasy, confided to a colleague, "A ship is not going to fire rockets at sea for nothing," sensing that something was badly wrong out there in the dark.

[1] British Wreck Commissioner's Inquiry, Encyclopedia Titanica.
[2] Robert D. Ballard, The Discovery of the Titanic (Toronto: Madison Press Books, 1987).
[3] Compton, Nic (2012). Titanic on Trial: The Night the Titanic Sank, Told Through the Testimonies of Her Passengers and Crew. Adlard Coles. p. 297

Part III—Aftermath

Chapter 7 — The Lost and the Living

To live is to suffer, to survive is to find some meaning in the suffering.

— Viktor Frankl

BY ABOUT 2:00 A.M., the ship's angle had become unmistakable. The bow had disappeared beneath the Atlantic, and the stern was rising behind it, slow but undeniable, lifting the long body of the ship out of its balance. Deck chairs slid toward the rail where they had rested for days. People leaned forward when they walked, instinctively bracing themselves against the pull of gravity. Inside the ship the strain was building in ways no one could see.

Titanic had been built to flex—to absorb the push and pull of a restless ocean—but not to carry the weight now dragging her forward. The flooded compartments in the bow pulled the great hull downward while the stern rose behind it, bending the ship across its middle. Steel groaned. Rivets strained. Deep below the waterline, forces were concentrating where the structure was weakest.

Edith Brown recalled the moment. "The bow seemed to sink more rapidly, and we could see the little forms on the deck running to the other end of the vessel, the instinct of self-preservation making them fight for those last minutes of life."

In the lifeboats, many people could not bear to watch.

"Then we turned our heads away," Edith recalled.

For a moment, the stern seemed to hesitate.

———————————◆———————————

Still standing on deck at 2:15 a.m. were third-class
passengers Rhoda Abbott and her two sons, Rossmore and
Eugene. They felt the moment as a strange interruption, not
a single thunderclap of breaking metal, but a violent
shudder that moved through the hull like a tremor through
the ground. Something had given way beneath them. They
jumped.[1]

The water struck like a blow. The cold of the Atlantic
was immediate and absolute, a shock that took the breath
from the lungs. Somewhere in the darkness nearby floated
Collapsible A, one of the ship's emergency boats that had
been launched too late and swamped by the sea as it came
off the deck.

Rhoda and the boys managed to reach it.

The boat was half-filled with freezing water, its sides
barely above the surface. Those who clung to it balanced
precariously along the edges. At first the night was full of
voices and splashing. Then, quietly, her boys disappeared.
Eugene went first. Then Rossmore. The cold took them
quickly.

As Edith Brown's lifeboat moved away from the ship, they
could still see Titanic, its rows of electric lights burning
steadily against the night. She would later remember the
moment with painful clarity. "As we rowed away from the
ship, we watched her," she later recalled. "the band was
playing a hymn; hardly had the strains of the hymn died
away from our ears before we could see that the mammoth

148

vessel was sinking slowly." From her vantage point in Lifeboat No. 11, Maude Slocombe recalled the band playing *Nearer My God To Thee.* The bow was lower now, the stern rising gradually into the dark sky.

"One by one the lights on the lower decks disappeared from sight," she said. "But those above the water were still burning."

Then, at approximately 2:18 a.m., they went out.

As the electrical systems on Titanic finally failed, the ship was plunged into darkness. The bow disappeared completely beneath the surface, pulling the broken forward section away and leaving the stern briefly afloat, isolated and vertical against the night sky. At around 2:20 a.m., Titanic began her final descent. Air escaped in bursts, and the last visible section slid beneath the surface of the Atlantic, and the sea closed over it.

The great liner was gone.

Illustration of Titanic's final moments

Then the sounds began.

"I could see nothing," Edith remembered, "but the shrieks and the screams that filled the air were terrible." As the ship vanished beneath the water a great sound rolled across the ocean—what she described as a long, terrible moan rising from hundreds of voices at once.

"I presume that it was just as she went under water that the most horrible moan as from a thousand lips came over the water… as that many men and I believe some women were hurled into the water and struggled about trying to find something on which to save themselves." For a moment after that sound, the sea went strangely still.

"After the awful moan it was quiet for a moment," she said. "And the screams broke out again."

No one in the boats knew what to say. Helen Churchill Candee later remembered the silence that followed the ship's disappearance. In the small circle of the lifeboat, words felt pointless beside the scale of what had just happened.

"No one spoke," she wrote later. "Speech was insufficient for such a catastrophe. The whole world was gone."

Hours later the lifeboats that had regrouped under Fifth Officer Harold Lowe began moving among the scattered survivors. Those still clinging to Collapsible A were eventually transferred to Collapsible D. Lowe supervised the rescue, making sure the living were brought aboard before the boats pulled away. Rhoda was pulled to safety.

Collapsible A drifted off into the darkness with three bodies still inside, their faces covered with lifebelts.

Later, a friend remembered the quiet way Rhoda spoke about the night. She said she was grateful that her boys had remained with her as long as they had on that piece of wreckage. The youngest went first, then the other. After that she remembered little. The cold had made everything numb.

What her friend did remember was a small detail from the rescue ship's cabin the next morning: a fragment of cork tangled in Rhoda's hair from the lifejacket she had worn in the water. It took a long time, working carefully with a comb, before they could pull it free.

A pocket watch retrieved from the wreck site, which stopped at 2:28

In the darkness beyond the ship, the lifeboats drifted together across the cold Atlantic. The oars moved slowly; everyone aboard sat in stunned silence.

In Lifeboat No. 14, Elizabeth Mellenger sat among the women in the boat, her daughter Violet close beside her. The night air had grown bitter. Around them coats and shawls were passed from one person to another as the cold worked its way through thin clothing meant for a warm April crossing.

At some point Second Officer Charles Lightoller reached their boat after escaping the ship. Exhausted and soaked from the freezing water, he was pulled aboard by the survivors. Elizabeth removed her cape and placed it around his shoulders, a small act of warmth in a boat where almost everyone was already shivering. Later, aboard Carpathia, Lightoller pressed his whistle into her hands in quiet thanks.

From the lifeboats drifting in the darkness, the passengers listened. What remained were lifeboats scattered across the dark water, debris spreading outward, and the sound—carried farther than sight ever could—of thousands of people suddenly left with nothing between themselves and the cold but the ocean itself.

The crossing was over. The waiting had ended.

April 15, Monday

Morning came slowly over the Atlantic. For those in the lifeboats, the first light did not bring comfort so much as clarity. The darkness that had hidden the ocean through the long night began to lift, and with it the survivors could finally see where they were.

Ice was everywhere.

Maude Slocombe later remembered that as the gray dawn spread across the water, the sea around the lifeboats revealed itself to be crowded with ice floes and towering icebergs. Some rose like pale cliffs from the still ocean, others drifted low and flat across the surface. In the cold morning light they seemed strangely beautiful—silent witnesses to the disaster that had unfolded among them only hours earlier.

The survivors realized then how close the ship had been to the danger.

Through the night they had heard warnings of ice. Now they could see it stretching across the horizon in every direction. The lifeboats floated among the same frozen landscape that had torn open the side of the great liner. It was there, in that cold field of drifting ice, that the survivors waited.

As dawn approached, Lifeboat No. 12 held nearly sixty people. Women pressed shoulder to shoulder, and crewmen balanced carefully at the oars. Mary Jane Sloan remained among them, one of the ship's stewardesses who had spent the night helping others before finally finding herself a passenger in the rescue.

Leah Aks also sat among sixty-three others; exhausted, numb, and hollowed by grief. Not long after sunrise, a thin column of smoke appeared on the horizon. Slowly it grew larger until the shape of a ship emerged from the morning haze.

The Carpathia was coming.

RMS Carpathia had received Titanic's distress calls after the signals were sent by Titanic's operators, Jack Phillips and Harold Bride. Carpathia immediately altered course and drove hard through ice fields, pushing her engines beyond their normal limits to reach the reported position as quickly as possible.

By approximately 4:00 a.m., Carpathia arrived at the scene.[2]

RMS Carpathia

What she encountered was unbelievable even to experienced and hardened seamen and crew. RMS Titanic was gone. In her place lay a scattered field of lifeboats drifting in the cold Atlantic; the sea calm but filled with debris and survivors clinging to what remained. The first lifeboat was brought alongside shortly after Carpathia's arrival, and rescue began at once.

Through the early morning, Carpathia worked steadily, boat by boat, hauling survivors aboard—many suffering from exposure, shock, or injury. Crew members distributed blankets and hot drinks, and makeshift medical spaces were set up to tend to the most severe cases. The work was methodical, urgent, and somber.

At 8:30 a.m., when the last lifeboat had been recovered and no further survivors could be found, Carpathia turned away from the wreck site. With all those she could save now aboard, she set her course westward toward New York City, carrying with her the living remnants of a ship that no longer existed.

❖

Aboard Carpathia

The first moments aboard Carpathia were not only moments of relief, but also of shock.

Survivors came up the ship's sides stiff with cold, hauled from lifeboats that had held them for hours in the dark.

Many could not stand without assistance. Some were barefoot. Others still wore nightclothes soaked with seawater. Nearly all were silent.

The rescue ship's passengers and crew had turned their lounges and dining rooms into temporary wards. Blankets were piled high. Thick, rough wool, wrapped around shoulders and heads. Hot drinks followed: tea, coffee, and soup. The warmth came slowly. Hands shook. Faces stared without focus. Some of the rescued spoke constantly, trying to explain what had happened in the dark hours before dawn. Others sat in silence, staring at nothing, the night still echoing in their minds. Rhoda Abbott was among the most badly affected.

After the freezing hours she had spent clinging to the wreckage of Collapsible A, the cold had settled deep into her body. Her legs were badly damaged from prolonged exposure to the icy water, and when she was brought aboard Carpathia, she could barely move.

She was laid on a padded sheet in the smoking room, now a makeshift infirmary, where she remained through the voyage to New York. Wrapped in blankets and tended by the ship's doctors and nurses, she drifted between exhaustion and numbness.[3]

When Carpathia reached New York on April 18, she was carried ashore and taken directly to a hospital, where she remained for at least two more weeks recovering from the effects of the freezing Atlantic.

Collapsible lifeboat D photographed from the deck of Carpathia on the morning of 15 April 1912.

As more Lifeboats appeared, names were recorded. Crew members and volunteers wrote them down carefully, sometimes asking twice, sometimes spelling phonetically when accents made clarity difficult. Survivors were asked where they had come from, which lifeboat they had been in, and whether they were alone or with someone else. For many, that question was the hardest to answer.

Some hesitated, unsure whether the people they were looking for were alive or merely late. Families, separated in the darkness, searched faces instinctively as each new group arrived: scanning for children, spouses, and siblings—hoping, even now, for a miracle.

That miracle came for Leah Aks who had spent the first days on Carpathia moving through the crowded decks and passageways, looking for her infant son, Filly. She searched the ship's makeshift wards and crowded cabins where they had gathered rescued women and children, without result.

Then, while standing on deck one morning, Leah heard a sound that cut through the noise of the ship—a baby's cry. It stopped her cold. In that instant, with a certainty that required no explanation, she knew the sound belonged to her son. Across the deck, a woman was holding an infant wrapped tightly in blankets. Leah hurried toward her and reached for the child, insisting the baby was hers. The woman refused to give him up. During the rescue's confusion, several infants boarded without clear identification, and she believed the child belonged with her.

The argument drew a small crowd.

At last the matter was brought before Captain Arthur Rostron. Leah pleaded her case, describing the child, the clothing he had worn, and the moment of their separation. Finally, she offered a detail that could not be mistaken: the strawberry birthmark on his chest. They examined the child. It was enough.

Phillip Franklin Aks was returned to his mother, ending one of the many quiet dramas that unfolded aboard the rescue ship as survivors slowly found their way back to the people they had lost in the darkness of the Atlantic.

Others weren't so fortunate.

Edith Brown and her mother found themselves that first day among the hundreds of survivors gathered in the ship's lounges and passageways, and they were searching.

Each time another lifeboat approached the side of the Carpathia, Edith ran to the railing, scanning the faces while the crew lifted the survivors aboard. In the gray morning light, every arriving boat carried the possibility that he might still be there. Someone told her he was. A man aboard the ship said he heard another lifeboat had saved her father. Edith held out hope.

It never materialized.

Years later, she remembered the long hours of waiting, the repeated rush to the rail whenever another boat appeared alongside. "When we were on board the Carpathia, a man told me that my father was in another boat," she said in 1912. "I don't know whether he knew him or not. Perhaps my father was in one of the overturned lifeboats."

Aboard the Carpathia, as the first shock of rescue gave way to the long voyage toward New York, the survivors slowly began to learn who among their fellow passengers had lived.

Lifeboat No. 14 rescued by Carpathia, including Elizabeth and Edith Brown and Elizabeth and Violet Mellenger

News traveled in fragments—one name at a time, passed quietly through the crowded lounges and passageways where the rescued gathered beneath borrowed blankets. Lists began to form in people's minds: those who had been seen in the boats, those who had not.

For Helen Churchill Candee, the news came in pieces about the small circle of men who had admired her aboard Titanic. Colonel Archibald Gracie had survived. He had endured the freezing water after the ship went down, clinging to the overturned collapsible lifeboat through the long night. Though he lived to tell the story, the ordeal had taken a lasting toll; many later believed that the shock and physical strain of that night contributed to his death the following year.

Then there was Woolner. He too had lived through the sinking, though survival had not brought him peace. Like many men pulled from the disaster, he carried the weight of having lived while so many others had not. The guilt of that knowledge followed him aboard the rescue ship, leaving little room to resume the easy companionship he and Helen had shared during the voyage.

Around them, the Carpathia moved steadily westward across the Atlantic, carrying with it not only the living, but also the fragile and incomplete accounting of who had been spared from the night Titanic disappeared.

They had survived the cold, the waiting, the fear of the sea—but now, safe for the first time, their bodies began to fail them. People fell asleep sitting upright. Others stared at the walls until they were gently guided elsewhere.

Inside, the work of recovering the living continued, repetitive and careful: blanket, drink, name, space. Again and again. Each arrival adding weight to the truth no one yet said aloud—that survival had not been evenly distributed, and that for many, rescue had come too late. And the quiet, disorienting realization that the ship that had carried them into the Atlantic was gone.

Seven hundred and five souls boarded the Carpathia. Nearly 1,500 had perished at sea.[4]

Who Survived, Who Did Not

But those 705 lives were not evenly distributed. Of the
women aboard Titanic, roughly three in four survived. In
first class, about 62 percent of women made it off the ship
alive. In second class, that number dropped to 41 percent.
In third class — down in the lower decks, behind the gates,
it was 25 percent. One in four.[5]

The order was women and children first. What it turned
out to mean was women and children of a certain deck, a
certain cabin number, a certain distance from the boats.
Class determined proximity to information, access to open
decks, and time. Those differences became decisive in the
last hours.

Colorized illustration of the iceberg thought to have been hit by
Titanic, original photograph was from the morning of 15 April
1912. Note the dark spot just along the berg's waterline, which
was described by onlookers as a smear of red paint thought to be
of a ship.

To understand what class actually cost you aboard Titanic, you have to strip away the other variables first. If sex and age were the only things that determined who lived and who died — if the ship had been, in that one sense, fair — then women across all classes would have had roughly a 74 percent chance of survival. Children, about 52 percent. Men, 20 percent. Those are the baseline numbers, applied evenly, without regard to which deck you slept on.

But on that night, they were not applied evenly.

When statisticians run the actual survivor counts against what those baseline odds would have predicted, the gap is stark. First-class passengers survived at a rate nearly 40 percent above what the math would have expected. Third-class passengers survived at a rate more than 30 percent below it. The difference between those two numbers is modest. The difference between what actually happened is not.

What filled that gap was not fate. It was the ship itself — its layout, its locked gates, its geography of privilege — working exactly as designed.

Of the 23 women working aboard Titanic as crew — 22 stewardesses and a matron — all but three survived. That 87 percent survival rate was among the highest of any group on the ship, a reflection of both the "women first" order and the simple fact that these women knew the ship, knew the decks, and didn't have to be told twice where the boats were.

They were not passengers. They had jobs to do, and most of them did those jobs until there was nothing left to do but get in a lifeboat.

Chaos in the Numbers: The First Reports

In the hours immediately following Titanic's sinking, a fog of confusion descended over the exact count of survivors. The wireless messages that crackled between ships and shore stations painted a wildly inconsistent picture, one that would take days to clarify.

The first wireless message reporting Titanic's distress came from the Carpathia at 1:40 AM on April 15th, stating simply: "Titanic struck iceberg, sinking fast." But it was the messages that followed, carrying conflicting survivor counts, that would create a rollercoaster of hope and despair for waiting families.

At 6:44 AM, a message from the Olympic reported optimistically that "All Titanic passengers safe." This false report, picked up by several newspapers, sparked premature celebrations in New York and Southampton. By afternoon, the Associated Press was reporting that Titanic was being towed to Halifax with all passengers safe - another cruel piece of early misinformation.

The Carpathia's wireless operator, Harold Cottam, worked tirelessly sending lists of survivors, but the task was overwhelming. Names were misspelled, particularly those of immigrant passengers. Some survivors gave different names than those on the passenger list, either out of confusion or fear. Third-class passengers, many speaking little or no English, had particular difficulty making their presence known.

The White Star Line offices in New York posted and revised survivor numbers throughout April 15th and 16th:

8:00 AM, April 15: "All passengers saved"

2:00 PM, April 15: "675 saved, mostly women and children"

6:00 PM, April 15: "866 rescued"

9:00 AM, April 16: "705 survivors confirmed"

People gathered in New York outside White Star Office

The confusion was compounded by several ships in the area receiving fragmentary wireless signals. The SS Frankfurt, SS Mount Temple, and RMS Baltic all reported different versions of events and varying survivor counts. The Baltic's captain even reported seeing Titanic still afloat at 10:50 AM on April 15th - a ghost signal that gave false hope to many.

Particularly heartbreaking were the scenes at the White Star Line offices, where families gathered desperately seeking information. Third-class families faced additional challenges as many of their names were mangled in wireless transmissions or omitted entirely from early reports. The wireless operators, working with limited technology and overwhelming message traffic, prioritized the names of first-class passengers in their transmissions.

It would not be until April 18th, when the Carpathia finally docked in New York, that a definitive count would emerge: 705 survivors out of 2,224 passengers and crew. The confusion of those first days, however, had already seared itself into the public consciousness, becoming part of the tragedy's lasting legacy.

A Tale of Two Arrivals

When the Carpathia finally docked at Pier 54 in New York on April 18th, 1912, the stark divisions of the Titanic continued to play out on American soil. The reception of survivors laid bare the social hierarchies that had shaped every aspect of the disaster.

First-Class Reception

As the Carpathia approached the pier, private cars and luxury hotels had already arranged for their wealthy clients. The Waldorf-Astoria, the Ritz-Carlton, and other prestigious establishments sent representatives to meet first-class survivors. John Jacob Astor IV's widow, Madeleine, was whisked away in a private limousine, while other elite passengers found refuge in the homes of New York's social elite.

The press eagerly sought interviews with first-class passengers, whose stories dominated newspaper headlines. Molly Brown, Bruce Ismay, and other prominent survivors received immediate medical attention from private physicians. Their accounts of the disaster were recorded in detail and preserved for history, with their names and experiences carefully documented.

Ned Parfett, "Titanic paperboy" outside the White Star Line offices at on Cockspur Street near Trafalgar Square in London. April 16, 1912.

The Press and Public Memory

In the days following the disaster, newspapers devoted countless columns to profiles of first-class passengers. The New York Times ran detailed accounts of the Astors, the

166

Strauses, and other prominent figures. But steerage passengers, when mentioned at all, were often reduced to numbers or nameless groups: "immigrants," "foreigners," "third-class passengers." Their individual stories, dreams, and sacrifices were largely ignored.

The rare exceptions usually involved heroism that served the upper classes. When steerage passenger Eugene Daly helped several first-class women into lifeboats, his story made the papers, though even then some accounts misspelled his name or confused his nationality.[6]

Second-Class Reception

Second-class passengers landed in a quieter kind of order. Aid societies and church groups had arranged rooms at mid-range hotels, and many survivors found their footing through a professional contact or a congregation that claimed them. Their stories made the papers too — just not the front page. They occupied the middle of the ship and, afterward, the middle of the coverage.

Steerage: The Forgotten Survivors

For steerage survivors, surviving the ship was only the first problem.

When they reached New York, many were taken directly to Ellis Island — the same gates, the same inspections, and the same lines they had been headed for before the collision. The disaster had not changed their paperwork. Officers processed them as they would have processed anyone arriving without money or connections or English, which is to say slowly, and with suspicion.

The financial assistance that reached first-class survivors quickly did not move the same way down the ladder. Relief funds existed, but navigating them required language, contacts, and a working knowledge of systems that had not been designed with a Croatian or Lebanese or Irish immigrant in mind. Many steerage survivors had lost everything below the waterline — their savings, their documents, the small objects that had made the crossing feel survivable. They arrived in America with what they had been wearing when they were pulled from the water.

The Hebrew Immigrant Aid Society, the Irish Emigrant Society, and others worked to fill the gap. They found cots in boarding houses, space in church basements, beds in settlement homes. It was not enough, and they knew it wasn't enough, and they kept working anyway.

The wealthy survivors told their stories from hotel suites and hospital beds, to reporters who spoke their language and knew how to write them down. The steerage survivors, when their accounts were recorded at all, came through interpreters, aid workers, and the filter of someone else's words. Which means that for many of them, the story of what they lived through never quite made it out.

The Crew's Reception

The surviving crew members faced their own challenges. While officers were treated similarly to second-class passengers, most of the 214 surviving crew members were taken to the Red Star Line's steamer SS Lapland, where they were accommodated in passenger cabins. Many were

quickly sent back to England, their stories untold and their
trauma unaddressed.

The Lost Voices

The White Star Line's offices were flooded with telegrams
and visitors seeking information about survivors, yet the
company's responses reflected the same class distinctions.
Inquiries about first-class passengers received prompt
attention, while families seeking information about steerage
passengers often waited days for any news.

This segregated reception foreshadowed how the
disaster would be remembered. The stories of wealthy
passengers would fill history books and shape the public
narrative, while the experiences of steerage passengers and
crew members often faded into obscurity, preserved mainly
in immigration records and aid society documents.

Many of Titanic's surviving passengers did not linger in
New York but immediately headed to relatives' homes.
What they carried back with them — the cold, the noise, the
particular silence of a lifeboat at 2 a.m. — would not be left
behind so easily. It would follow them home, and stay.

[1] Eaton, John P.; Haas, Charles A. (1987). Titanic: Destination Disaster: The Legends and the Reality.
[2] Walter Lord, A Night to Remember (New York: Henry Holt and Company, 1955), 188–195.
[3] Charles Pellegrino, Her Name, Titanic (New York: McGraw-Hill, 1988).
[4] Gittins, Dave; Akers-Jordan, Cathy; Behe, George (2011). "Too Few Boats, Too Many Hindrances". In Halpern, Samuel (ed.). Report into the Loss of the SS Titanic: A Centennial Reappraisal. Stroud, Gloucestershire: The History Press.
[5] British Board of Trade. Titanic Disaster: Official Casualty Figures and Commentary. London: His Majesty's Stationery Office, 1912.
[6] "Eugene Patrick Daly," Encyclopedia Titanica.

Chapter 8 — Inquiries, Legacy, and Lost Voices

Believe those who are seeking the truth. Doubt those who find it.

— André Gide

WITHIN HOURS OF CARPATHIA'S arrival in New York, two nations began preparing for what would become the most extensive maritime investigations of their time. The parallel inquiries - one American, one British - would reveal not only the circumstances of Titanic's sinking, but also the deeply rooted problems in the shipping industry itself.

American Investigation

The American investigation that Senator William Alden Smith of Michigan launched was conducted with unprecedented speed, beginning just one day after Carpathia docked. He understood, correctly, that witnesses scatter, memories harden and shipping companies have lawyers.

The hearings opened at the elegant Waldorf-Astoria and later moved to the Senate Office Building. Smith called everyone he could get: surviving officers, crew members, passengers from all three classes, executives from White Star Line. What he got, depending on who was in the chair, were very different kinds of testimony.

First-class passengers and senior officers testified in the same rooms where they might otherwise have taken dinner. Crew members arrived still in borrowed clothes, some not yet fully out of shock, and were questioned with a sharpness that did not much account for what they had just been through. Steerage survivors who spoke little or no English were filtered through interpreters, their accounts already losing something in translation before they reached the record.

Second Officer Charles Lightoller sat before the committee and became its central figure. When Smith pressed him on the ship's speed through ice-warning waters, Lightoller fell back on a phrase he would use more than once: it was common practice. Smith asked whether common practice and safe practice were the same thing. Lightoller's answer did not quite say yes, and did not quite say no, and that, too, went into the record.

The British Board of Trade Inquiry

While the American investigation was still ongoing, the British Board of Trade launched its own inquiry under Lord Mersey.

Beginning on May 2, 1912, at the Scottish Drill Hall in London, this investigation took a markedly different approach. Where the American inquiry had been broad and sometimes sensational, the British hearings were technical and focused.

Yet here too, class and title played a role. Officers were addressed by their titles and questioned with a kind of professional courtesy, one set of men in suits talking to another. Crew members from the lower decks got something closer to an interrogation. Several of them said afterward that the formal atmosphere — the marble, the stenographers, the lawyers — had made them feel less like witnesses than suspects.

Then Frederick Fleet sat down.

Fleet had been in the crow's nest the night of April 14th, one of the two lookouts responsible for seeing what was coming. He told the committee that he had no binoculars. They had been left behind in Southampton — an oversight, a miscommunication, a small administrative failure that had preceded one of the largest maritime disasters in history. Senator Smith asked Fleet whether binoculars might have helped him spot the iceberg sooner.

"Yes, sir," Fleet said. Two words. A small item. Whether true or not, the record remains.

Key Findings and Contradictions

Both inquiries arrived at the same place, more or less, differing only in how much they were willing to say out loud. The core conclusion was clear: the ship did not have to sink. What happened on April 14th was not an act of nature in any meaningful sense. It was the result of human decisions, made over months and years and hours, stacked one on top of another until the weight of them broke through the hull.

Titanic had steamed into known ice fields at full speed, or close to it, despite repeated warnings. The warnings had come in by wireless, had been noted, and had not meaningfully changed anything. Schedule mattered. Prestige mattered. The idea that this ship in particular could not be seriously threatened by ordinary hazards mattered most of all. Ice was treated as weather — an inconvenience to be logged and pressed through rather than a condition that demanded a different kind of attention.

The lifeboats could hold barely half the people aboard. This was not a secret, and it was not illegal. It was simply the standard, and no one with the authority to change it had seen reason to do so before the night it became relevant.

The crew had not drilled together for a full evacuation. Emergency procedures existed on paper in ways they did not exist in practice, and when the order finally came, it moved unevenly through the ship — different instructions on different decks, officers making judgment calls in the dark, passengers receiving word late or not at all. The wireless operators, for all the modernity of their equipment, were understaffed and poorly coordinated. Distress calls went out and were missed, or heard and misread, narrowing the window for rescue in ways that didn't have to happen.

And then there was the finding that sat beneath all the others, the one both inquiries circled but only partially named: that where you slept on that ship largely determined whether you lived or died. Not fate. Not the iceberg. But the description of your ticket.

The lifeboats, information, and the hands that helped — none of it moved evenly through the ship. Some third-class passengers were physically blocked from reaching the boat deck. Others were stopped by locked gates, by corridors that led nowhere useful, by instructions shouted in a language they didn't speak. By the time many of them found their way up, the boats were going or gone.

Both inquiries acknowledged this. Neither pressed it as hard as the facts warranted. What they did conclude, clearly enough, was that the dead were not simply victims of an iceberg. They were victims of a social order that had boarded the ship in Southampton and refused to loosen its grip even as the stern rose out of the water. An order that prioritized hierarchy and appearances and the comfort of the right kind of passenger over the basic urgency of getting people off a sinking hull.[1]

On the ship itself, the inquiry did not rule that Titanic was inherently defective in her build; instead it emphasized the limits of contemporary design assumptions—how watertight subdivision, though advanced, still had boundaries that the iceberg's damage exceeded. The report's recommendations pushed for more substantial safety margins in construction and equipment going forward.

Wireless, too, was exposed as a system with modern power but old protocols. The inquiry dealt with practicalities—how wireless was staffed and used, and how distress and ice information could fail to move with the urgency the situation demanded—leading to calls for tighter expectations around wireless vigilance and procedure so warnings and emergencies could not be lost in routine traffic.

Impact on Maritime Safety

The findings did not remain ink on paper. They led to sweeping changes in maritime safety regulations and hardened into an international safety regime designed to prevent a single ship's choices from becoming a mass grave again.

Time to get busy by Fisher, 1912. Public outrage at the disaster led politicians to impose new regulations on the shipping industry. By "Fisher" - St. Louis Republic via Marshall Everett, Story of the Wreck of the Titanic.

In 1914, governments convened the first International Convention for the Safety of Life at Sea (SOLAS) to establish minimum standards for construction, equipment, and operation across national boundaries. One of SOLAS's clearest responses to Titanic was arithmetic, not rhetoric:

ships were expected to provide lifeboat accommodation for everyone aboard.

Alongside that came the insistence that help could not depend on chance listening—continuous watch on distress and safety frequencies became the expectation, and radio vigilance became part of the safety system rather than a commercial convenience.

The ocean itself was also put under watch. The International Ice Patrol, operating from 1914 onward, institutionalized what had been improvised and unreliable: coordinated iceberg surveillance and warnings for North Atlantic shipping lanes.

Onboard, the new requirements evolved into regular emergency training and drills—not just for the crew but also for passengers, with musters expected early in a voyage—so an evacuation would be a practiced procedure rather than first-time chaos.

Design and operations shifted in parallel, though not always as a single, universal mandate. After Titanic, ships were retrofitted and redesigned with stronger subdivision assumptions—bulkheads were extended higher on some vessels, double-bottom protection was expanded, and emergency systems (lighting, signaling, life-saving equipment standards) became central engineering considerations rather than optional upgrades.[2]

And while laws cannot erase social prejudice overnight, the post-Titanic reforms advanced a simple principle: in an emergency, procedures must be clear, well-drilled, and applicable to everyone on board—because the sea does not recognize class, language, or status. However, it would take decades for this principle to be fully implemented.

The Fading of Faces: How Steerage Was Erased from Memory

While the inquiries were underway in America and Britain, another event was unfolding between them in the icy Atlantic waters—the recovery of bodies.

When the scale of the disaster became undeniable, the recovery of the dead was entrusted to corporate and administrative decisions, which were once again shaped by class.

White Star Line chartered the cable ship CS Mackay-Bennett from Halifax, followed by several other Canadian vessels, each stocked with embalming supplies, undertakers, and clergy. What followed was not a neutral humanitarian operation, but a triage that reflected whose lives—and bodies—were deemed worth preserving.

The Mackay-Bennett reached the wreck site first and was immediately overwhelmed. Bodies outnumbered supplies. Faced with limited embalming materials and strict health regulations that barred the return of unembalmed remains to port, the ship's captain and undertakers made a consequential decision: priority would be given to preserving the remains of first-class passengers.

The justification was practical on its face—wealthy victims needed to be visually identified to settle estates—but its effect was unmistakable. Dozens of third-class passengers and crew were committed to the sea, their bodies deliberately left unrecovered. In death, as in life, class dictated treatment.

The process was methodical. Recovered bodies were numbered, measured, and cataloged. Clothing, physical features, and personal effects were logged with care. The purser locked away the valuables. But the system itself required choices. Clothing was sometimes used to classify bodies as crew. Burial at sea was framed as a sailor's fate—an acceptable end—but this rationale fell almost exclusively on those with the least social standing aboard.

The bodies were brought back to Halifax, where they had converted a curling rink into a morgue. A small army of clerks and officials built identification systems from scratch. Families came from across North America to walk the rows. About two-thirds of the recovered dead received identification. They buried the rest under markers that assigned them only a number.

Of the 333 bodies pulled from the North Atlantic — one in five of the more than 1,500 who died out there — the majority interred were third-class passengers and crew. Their headstones are uniform. Small, flat, identical. The lives beneath them were not.

The pattern held to the end. Bodies recovered in the later weeks — some drifting hundreds of miles from the wreck site, others still in the deteriorating hull of Collapsible A — were frequently buried at sea without ceremony, without record, without anyone to object. The last body recovered was a ship's steward. He was given a number and buried quietly in Halifax, and that was that.

By June, the search vessels were reporting that life jackets were breaking down in the water, releasing what they had held. The ocean was taking back its evidence. The cold arithmetic of the disaster — who was saved, who was not, and why — was already passing from fact into history. For many in third class, there was no return home, no funeral attended by family, no name carved in stone.

The Language of Loss

Even the vocabulary used to describe the dead revealed the class divisions. First-class passengers were "lost," while steerage passengers were "drowned." Wealthy victims were "claimed by the sea," while poor ones "went down with the ship." These subtle linguistic differences reinforced the notion that some lives - and deaths - mattered more than others.

Memorials and Monuments

Physical memorials to Titanic's dead tell an equally stark story. In Southampton, where many crew members lived, the memorial lists officers by name but refers to most crew members simply as "crew. Initially, the Belfast memorial, erected where Titanic was built, listed only prominent passengers and crew. It wasn't until 2020 that a supplementary plaque was added, acknowledging the steerage passengers who died; a belated recognition of this historical oversight.

Missing Names

The ship's hierarchy didn't end at the waterline. It followed the dead into the record books.

Nearly every first-class passenger who sailed on Titanic can be accounted for today — photographed, biografied, their cabin numbers and dinner companions and last known movements reconstructed with the kind of detail usually reserved for heads of state. Ninety-eight percent of them, fully documented. Second-class passengers fare somewhat worse, about three in four with basic biographical information attached to their names.

For steerage, fewer than half have been verified with full names and confirmed backgrounds. The rest exist in the record as fragments — a name spelled three different ways across different manifests, a hometown that no longer exists under that name, a family that arrived in America and changed everything about themselves in order to survive it. Some of those identities will never be fully recovered. The language barriers that slowed them on the boat deck followed them into history.

What gets documented, gets remembered. What gets remembered, gets mourned properly, and gets a headstone with a name on it rather than a number. The disparity was not accidental. It was the ledger of a world that had already decided, long before the iceberg, whose stories were worth keeping.[3]

The Preservation of Objects

Even in museums, this disparity persists. Artifacts from first-class cabins — china, jewelry, furniture — were carefully preserved and displayed. But few objects from steerage survived, and even fewer were deemed worthy of preservation.

In recent years, efforts have been made to rectify this historical imbalance. Genealogists and historians have worked to reconstruct the stories of third-class passengers, and projects such as the Titanic Heritage Trust have focused explicitly on documenting third-class passengers and crew members.

Digital databases now aim to tell the complete story of everyone who sailed on the Titanic, regardless of class. Yet the century-long gap in documentation leaves many stories incomplete or lost entirely. The erasure that began in 1912 created historical blind spots that can never be fully corrected.

[1] Report on the Loss of the S.S. Titanic, British Wreck Commissioner's Inquiry, July 30, 1912.

[2] Butler, Daniel Allen (1998). Unsinkable: the full story of the RMS Titanic (1st ed.). Mechanicsburg, PA: Stackpole Books

[3] Eaton, John P.; Haas, Charles (1996). Titanic: Destination Disaster. W. W. Norton & Company.

Chapter 9—After the Waves: Lives Reshaped by Survival

You must do the thing you think you cannot do.

— Eleanor Roosevelt

THE PHYSICAL RESCUE FROM Titanic's icy waters marked only the beginning of a much longer journey for survivors. The disaster's impact would echo through their lives for decades, reshaping futures in vastly different ways depending on their social class and circumstances.

Support networks emerged, though they too reflected the ship's class divisions. Immigrant survivors created their own informal support systems within their communities. In New York's Lower East Side, a group of Jewish survivors met regularly at a local synagogue, sharing their experiences in Yiddish and helping each other navigate their new lives in America.

When it came time to settle the financial claims, White Star Line did what the ship itself had done: it sorted by class. First-class losses were handled quickly and generously, and were offered settlements that acknowledged that the people on the other side of the table had lawyers of their own and connections that made prolonged disputes uncomfortable. Second-class passengers received something more modest, after negotiations that stretched longer than they should have. Steerage passengers, if they received anything at all, got the minimum — settlements that bore little relationship to what had actually been lost, which, in many cases was everything. Crew families fought for basic compensation the way you fight when you have no leverage and everyone on the other side of the table knows it.

The ship had taken three hours to sink. The paperwork took considerably longer, and arrived at roughly the same conclusion: that some lives, priced out, were worth more than others.

Helen Candee

Helen was rescued by Carpathia with a broken ankle — an injury that would keep her on a cane for nearly a year — but she was working before the ship that saved her had docked. Within weeks of the sinking, Collier's Weekly ran her account, "*Sealed Orders,*" on its cover, accompanied by photographs taken aboard Carpathia of survivors still wearing the stunned expressions of people who had not yet fully processed what they had survived. It was one of the first major eyewitness accounts published anywhere.

Helen went on, as she always had. She wrote, traveled, and continued the career she had been building long before she booked passage on Titanic. She outlasted most of the people she had known that night. In 1949, at ninety years old, she died at her summer cottage at York Harbor, Maine.

Edith Rosenbaum

Edith Rosenbaum had carried a toy pig off a sinking ship, the world would never forget it. She gave interviews about it for decades, and the pig became the thing people remembered, which may or may not have suited her.

She retired from the fashion world around 1937 but kept moving — traveling extensively into old age, impossible to keep still. The National Maritime Museum eventually displayed the pig and the slippers she wore in the lifeboat; objects that had crossed the Atlantic on the worst night in the history of ocean travel and come out the other side intact.

In 2001, James Cameron's expedition to the wreck found her first-class cabin largely as she had left it. The dressing-table mirror was still upright. Still intact. Photographs of the room were published in the 2003 book *Ghosts of the Abyss*. Somewhere in the deep, in the dark, in a ship that had been on the ocean floor for nearly ninety years, her room had held its shape.

She would have appreciated that.

Elizabeth and Edith Brown

Elizabeth and Edith Brown waited in New York for days after Carpathia docked, unwilling to leave while any possibility of news about the fate of their husband and father remained.

But he had not made it off the ship. No word ever came. Eventually, they did what the bereaved do when waiting becomes its own kind of cruelty — they continued west, alone, carrying what they had left.

They returned to Cape Town, and then to Australia. By 1914, they had settled in Johannesburg. Edith carried the Titanic quietly for decades. Her first public return to it came in 1958, when she attended a screening of *A Night to Remember* and met several other survivors, among them

Millvina Dean, with whom she would remain close for the rest of her life. From the late 1970s onward, as public appetite for Titanic history intensified, so did the calls on Edith's time. She gave interviews to television, radio, and local newspapers. She attended conventions in Britain and the United States, eventually in a wheelchair, frail but present, still willing to tell it.

In 1993, someone placed her father's pocket watch in her hands. It had been recovered from the ocean floor by an expedition team — pulled up from the wreck after eighty years in the dark. She was in her nineties. The watch had been with her father when the ship went down, and now it was with her again.

Some things find their way back.

Elizabeth and Violet Mellenger

They left the ship together and stayed together. That much, at least, the night gave them.

Elizabeth and Violet Mellenger were among the many mothers and daughters who made their way up through the confusion of those last hours, following instructions, trusting that the wooden boats being lowered into the dark below would hold.

After the sinking, they returned to England, then emigrated to Canada around 1915, settling in Toronto and building the quiet life Elizabeth had presumably been crossing the Atlantic to find in the first place. She found it, more or less. But she carried the ship with her.

Elizabeth Anne Mellenger died on January 4th, 1962, and is buried in St. John's Ridgeway Cemetery near Welland, Ontario. She had been trying to get there her whole life.

Rhoda Abbott

She stayed until the end because her boys were there. That was all. No hesitation, no calculation — just a mother who was not going to leave the ship while her sons were still on it. Rhoda Abbott was the only woman survivor known to have gone into the water that night rather than off in a lifeboat. She was pulled from the North Atlantic alive. Her sons, Rossmore and Eugene, were not. The Providence Evening Bulletin ran the headline with the particular cruelty of newspaper matter-of-factness: *Two Providence Boys Added to Titanic Lost.*

She had stayed on the ship for them, but survived without them. She had no regrets about her decision; she said later that it had allowed her more time with them. Whether the surviving made sense took longer to answer.

On December 16th, 1912 — eight months after the sinking — Rhoda married George Charles Williams, a former lodger, in Swansea, Massachusetts. It was the kind of quiet, practical decision that grief sometimes produces: someone who already knew her, who was already there. They settled in Jacksonville, Florida, where George worked as a bookbinder. In 1928, they returned to England, and Rhoda remained in their home in Barnes, Surrey, until her death on February 18th, 1946.

In the ship's final record for Lifeboat No. 11 he was listed with the economy of a ledger entry: *AKS, Master Philip. 10 months. 3rd Class Passenger.* Ten months old, third class, Lifeboat 11, one name.

When Leah and Filly reached Norfolk, Sam was waiting. Life resumed and filled in around what had happened. A daughter was born on March 12th, 1913, and they named her Sarah Carpathia — after the ship, after the rescue, after the night the ocean gave Filly back. A son, Harry, followed in January 1915. The family settled in Norfolk, where Leah became a fixed presence in the local Jewish community. She was the kind of woman who showed up, who joined, and who stayed. Local media called on her regularly to tell her Titanic story, and she did. In the 1950s, when public interest in the disaster reawakened, she attended screenings of Fox's *Titanic* and *A Night to Remember* as a guest of honor, watching the ship go down again from a theater seat.

She became reacquainted with other survivors over the years — Thelma Thomas, May Futrelle, Selena Cook, and Salini Yazbak Decker, among them. She and Mrs. Decker eventually discovered that they had been living within blocks of each other in Norfolk for years without knowing it. Two women from the same ship, the same night, the same cold water — neighbors, all along.

Leah Aks died on June 22nd, 1967, at Norfolk General Hospital. She was seventy-six. Sam survived her by three years, dying on November 11th, 1970. Her son, the baby in the record, died in 1991. His name was Philip. They called him Filly. He landed in a stranger's arms and lived.

When Titanic went down, she got herself off it, made it onto Carpathia, crossed to New York, and then turned around and sailed back to England aboard the Lapland. Back to work. Back to life. That was Maude.

She remained a masseuse for years afterward, and later a housekeeper — the kind of woman who was always in service to something, always useful, always in the room but rarely the center of it. She eventually settled in New York, in the Bronx, though she never lost the Cockney accent she had carried over from London. Decades in America and it stayed with her, intact, the way certain things do.

In the 1950s, Walter Lord wrote to her as part of his research for *A Night to Remember*, and she wrote back. Her anecdotes made it into the book — her voice, her details, her particular view from below decks preserved in the margins of someone else's account, which is where crew members so often end up.

Maude Slocombe died in the Bronx on July 30th, 1967, one day before her eighty-sixth birthday. She had outlasted the ship by fifty-five years, which would have seemed, on the night of April 14th, 1912, like an impossible number. She made it look easy.

Mary Jane Sloan

After Titanic, Mary Jane Sloan went back to sea. That alone says everything about her. She had survived crises aboard two separate ships, two accidents, and when she returned to Belfast in late May 1912, she did not stay ashore. She went back. Some people are built that way — not reckless, exactly, but unwilling to let what happened at sea become the thing that defines what happens on land.

What she thought about all of it, no one knows. In the decades that followed, as other survivors gave interviews, attended screenings, corresponded with researchers, and told their stories to anyone who would listen, Mary Jane Sloan said nothing. Not one recorded interview or a single public account. Whatever she carried from that night she kept to herself, which in its own way is as striking as anything she might have said.

She died in 1953, aged eighty-six. She is buried in Dundonald Cemetery in an unmarked grave. No ceremony, no attention, no retrospective notice from a press that had long since moved on. She had been on one of the most written-about ships in history and she left no trace of having said a word about it. Some silences are louder than testimony.

Titanic on the Atlantic Ocean Floor

Closing Thoughts

Titanic is remembered for its grandeur and its horror, for the iceberg and the band and the millionaires in their smoking jackets. The record shows something quieter and harder to look at. Titanic was a system, and it wasn't designed to protect everyone the same.

It was written into the corridors, the gate locks, and the distance between a third-class berth and the boat deck. It determined who received clear instructions and who received none, who had a steward at their cabin door and who had to find their own way up through a ship they had never been shown. When the systems failed, those divisions did not soften. They hardened. The ocean was indifferent. The ship was not.

None of this is a relic of 1912. Industrial accidents, environmental disasters, pandemics — the same fault lines appear, every time, with a consistency that cannot be called coincidence. Essential workers absorb the risk. Marginalized communities absorb the losses. Accountability, afterward, has a way of dissolving into inquiry, report, and recommendation, until the next time.

Titanic endures not because it was exceptional but because it was legible. Everything that went wrong went wrong in a way that left a record — the wireless logs, the testimony, the survivor lists sorted by class. It is one of the rare disasters that documented its own inequity in real time, and handed it to history still warm.

The warning it carries is not about icebergs. It is about what gets built into a system before the crisis comes, about who is protected by design and who is protected as an afterthought, if at all. Technology did not save the people in steerage. Procedure did not save them. The modern world, in all its confidence, did not save them.

What the women shared was not heroism in any dramatic sense, not the kind that gets a statue or a headline. They all shared the morning after. The lifeboat reaching Carpathia. The gangplank in New York. The telegram that had to be sent, or received. The decisions, made quietly and without ceremony, to continue.

Some of them talked about it for the rest of their lives. Others never said another word. Some named their children after the ship that saved them. Others went straight back to sea. Some walked with a cane for a year and then put it away. Some carried it in their bodies, in dreams we have no record of because no one thought to ask.

Titanic has never stopped sinking, not really. It goes down fresh for every generation that finds it — in books, in films, in the cold arithmetic of the survivor lists. What gets lost in the retelling, what gets smoothed over by the myth of it, is the specific weight of specific lives. The stewardess who kept her accent. The mother who stayed for her sons and came up without them. The baby thrown into the dark and caught. The woman who went back to sea, or the woman who said nothing, ever, and took it all with her to an unmarked grave.

They were not symbols. They were people, which is harder to hold onto but more important to try.

The ship is still down there. Two and a half miles down, in water that is just above freezing, in a darkness that has not lifted in over a hundred years. It is going slowly back to the ocean that took it — the hull collapsing inward, the staterooms filling with sediment, the grand staircase long gone. James Cameron's cameras found Edith Russell's mirror still standing on its dressing table. Someday it will not be standing. Someday there will be nothing left but a stain on the ocean floor, a shadow in the sediment where something large and certain once believed it could not sink.

They got in the boats. They kept going. That is the whole story, and it is enough.

Acknowledgements

This book rests on the work of countless historians, archivists, librarians, and researchers who have spent more than a century preserving the records of Titanic—often fragmentary, sometimes contradictory, always human. Passenger lists, inquiry transcripts, letters, affidavits, newspapers, and family histories made it possible to move beyond legend and return names, context, and consequence to those too often reduced to statistics.

I am especially indebted to the modern scholars and independent researchers who continue to question inherited narratives, challenge class-blind retellings, and recover overlooked communities—immigrants, crew, laborers, and families whose experiences shaped the disaster but rarely shaped its mythology. Their insistence on evidence over romance has guided the tone and structure of this work.

Finally, this book owes a quiet debt to the passengers and crew themselves. Many left little behind beyond a name, a testimony, or a single remembered act. To treat those fragments with care—to resist embellishment while honoring meaning—has been the central obligation of this project. Any errors remain my own.

Notes on Sources

This book draws on a layered record: official investigations, contemporary reporting, ship documentation, survivor testimony, and later scholarship that re-examines the evidence with modern methods. Where sources conflict—as they often do in Titanic history—I have prioritized contemporaneous documents and clearly attributable statements over later retellings. When a detail is widely repeated but weakly sourced, I either omit it or frame it explicitly as uncertain.

Primary and Near-Primary Sources

The backbone of the factual narrative comes from the two official post-disaster investigations: the United States Senate Inquiry (1912) and the British Wreck Commissioner's Inquiry (the "Mersey Report," 1912). These records preserve sworn testimony, timelines, and operational details—ice warnings, speed, lifeboat handling, wireless practices, and crew procedure. They are indispensable for understanding what happened and how authorities interpreted accountability in the immediate aftermath.

I also rely on contemporaneous ship and corporate documentation where available: passenger lists, crew lists, deck plans and technical specifications, and wireless logs or summaries of wireless traffic. For individual lives, I use letters, postcards, affidavits, and family documents when they can be traced to an archive or reputable scholarly publication.

Newspapers and Contemporary Periodicals

Newspapers from April–June 1912 provide immediacy—names, early survivor interviews, public reaction, and the evolving "first draft" of events. They are also a minefield: rushed reporting, hearsay, and sensational framing were common. I use newspapers primarily to capture contemporary language and public perception, and I cross-check claims against inquiry testimony or later vetted scholarship before treating them as fact.

Modern Scholarship and Curated Databases

For passenger biographies, demographics, and cross-referenced survival outcomes, I rely on established reference works and curated research databases maintained by long-standing Titanic historians and institutions. These resources are valuable for aggregation—nationality, port of embarkation, family groupings, and post-disaster lives—but they still require caution. "Nationality," for example, can mean citizenship, birthplace, ethnicity, or modern national identity; I indicate the definition used when it matters.

Reconstructing Everyday Life Onboard

Details about daily routines—third-class spaces, meal service, rules around movement between decks, and steerage conditions—come from a combination of ship plans, company practices on contemporary liners, and survivor accounts. When I describe "what a day likely looked like," I anchor the scene in these broader, well-documented patterns rather than inventing specific actions or dialogue.

Handling Uncertainty and Anecdote

Some of the most compelling Titanic stories are also the least reliable. In this book, anecdotal material is included only when it is traceable to a named witness, a published memoir/interview with clear provenance, or a well-regarded scholarly work that cites underlying documentation. When a story is memorable but unverified, it is treated as a reported tradition—not as fact.

Citations and Verification

Citations are provided to allow readers to follow the evidence. Where possible, I cite primary sources first, then the best modern synthesis. If you are using this book as a research starting point, the inquiry transcripts and contemporary documentation should be your first stop; modern works are most useful for context, cross-checking, and locating scattered primary material.

About the Author

Alina Rush is neither a Titanic specialist nor a maritime historian. Like countless others, her interest in the ship and its sinking grew from a lifelong fascination—one shaped by memory, repetition, and the unanswered questions that cling to the disaster more than a century later. What drew her to this project was not the mythology of Titanic but the people who lived and worked within it and the way so many of their stories have faded beneath familiar headlines.

Rush brings more than twenty-five years of experience crafting narratives for marginalized communities worldwide. Her work has focused on restoring context, dignity, and voice to lives often reduced to footnotes or stereotypes.

She is also the daughter of immigrants who made their own harrowing journeys to America aboard ocean liners like Titanic in the early twentieth century. This book is written in recognition that migration, labor, and loss were not abstractions—they were lived realities carried across the Atlantic by ordinary people whose hopes were larger than the ships that carried them.

A Note from the Author

If this book helped you see Titanic differently—less as a legend, more as a lived experience—I would be grateful if you shared your experience by leaving a review. Reviews matter not as praise, but as signals to other readers that these stories are worth encountering. Even a brief, honest review helps keep books like this visible.

This title is part of a larger body of work published by Unbound Press, dedicated to overlooked histories, marginalized voices, and rigorously researched nonfiction. If this approach resonates with you, I invite you to explore the full catalog. Each book asks a similar question: whose stories were carried forward, and whose were left behind?

More titles like this are available at www.UnboundPressBooks.com.

Thank you for reading—and for helping these histories continue to be read.

More Books by <u>Unbound Press</u> are available at
www.unboundpressbooks.com

Frontier Chronicles: *Stories of the Contested American Frontier*

<u>Ghost Dance War</u>
The Last Uprising of Native Nations

<u>Women on the Prairie</u>
Stories of Grit, Survival, and Unbroken Spirit

Spirits Unbroken: *Indigenous America Series*

<u>Echoes from the Eastern Shore</u>
Twelve Native American Chiefs and the Fight for the
Atlantic Homelands

Last Council Fires (coming soon)
Twelve Chiefs of the Colonial Southeast

Fault Lines: *Titanic Micro-histories*

<u>Steerage and Steel</u>
The True Story of Titanic's Crew and Immigrants

Ladies First
Titanic's Reckoning with Wealth and Worth

<u>American Silencer</u>
A History of Political Violence in America

America Uncovered

Appendix

Lifeboats: Lifeboat Tally

Boat 1 — 12 aboard

Boat 2 — 18 aboard

Boat 3 — 32 aboard

Boat 4 — 30 aboard

Boat 5 — 36 aboard

Boat 6 — 24 aboard

Boat 7 — 28 aboard

Boat 8 — 27 aboard

Boat 9 — 40 aboard

Boat 10 — 57 aboard

Boat 11 — 50 aboard

Boat 12 — 41 aboard

Boat 13 — 55 aboard

Boat 14 — 40 aboard

Boat 15 — 66 aboard

Boat 16 — 52 aboard

Boat A — 13 aboard

Boat B — 28 aboard

Boat C — 43 aboard

Boat D — 20 aboard

Total persons saved by lifeboats: 712

Emergency Lifeboat 1 (Starboard)

Launch time: Approximately 1:10 a.m.

Officer(s) in charge: First Officer William Murdoch; Fifth Officer Harold Lowe; Lookout George Symons (placed in command)

Rated capacity: 40 persons

Estimated number aboard at launch: 12

Emergency Lifeboat 1 was the first of Titanic's two emergency cutters to be launched with only 12 aboard: seven crew members and five First Class passengers.

The composition of the boat reflected Murdoch's discretionary interpretation of "women and children first," under which married couples and individual men had already been permitted to board other lifeboats. Several first-class male passengers were allowed to board with Murdoch's consent. Murdoch also directed several crewmen to enter the boat and placed Lookout George Symons in command.

After the Titanic sank, the boat did not return to attempt water rescues. Later testimony conflicted as to whether such a return was proposed or discussed among those aboard.

RMS Carpathia recovered Emergency Lifeboat 1.

Selected occupants:

– George Symons, Lookout (in command)

– Sir Cosmo Duff-Gordon and his wife, Lucy

– Laura Mabel Francatelli

Emergency Lifeboat 2 (Port)

Launch time: Approximately 1:45 a.m.

Officer(s) in charge: Captain Edward J. Smith; Chief Officer Henry Wilde; Fourth Officer Joseph Groves Boxhall (placed in command)

Rated capacity: 40 persons

Estimated number aboard at launch: Approximately 18

Emergency Lifeboat 2, the second of Titanic's two cutters, departed carrying only about 18 persons, primarily women, along with one male third-class passenger who boarded to accompany his wife and young child.

After Titanic sank, Fourth Officer Boxhall proposed returning to rescue people in the water, but the occupants refused.

At approximately 4:00 a.m., Boxhall sighted RMS Carpathia on the horizon and fired a green flare to signal the ship. Emergency Lifeboat 2 became the first lifeboat to reach Carpathia, arriving at approximately 4:10 a.m.

RMS Carpathia recovered Emergency Lifeboat 2 at approximately 4:10 a.m.

Selected occupants:

– Joseph Groves Boxhall, Fourth Officer (in command)

– Anton Kink, with his wife Louise and daughter

– Charlotte Appleton

– Mallvina Cornell

– Minnie Coutts and her sons William and Neville

Lifeboat 3 (Starboard)

Launch time: Approximately 1:00 a.m.

Officer(s) in charge: First Officer William Murdoch; Fifth Officer Harold Lowe; Able Seaman George Moore (placed in command)

Rated capacity: 65 persons

Estimated number aboard at launch: Approximately 32

As with earlier launches, many passengers did not fully grasp the seriousness of the situation. Railroad executive Charles Melville Hays escorted his wife, daughter, and maid into the boat but did not attempt to board. Contemporary accounts describe the embarkation at this time as calm and orderly, with little outward panic.

Survivors described the atmosphere on deck during the launch as formal and almost unreal. The ship's band continued to play, and passengers reportedly laughed and conversed as the boats were lowered.

Lifeboat 3 was rescued by RMS Carpathia at approximately 7:30 a.m.

Selected occupants:

– George Moore, Able Seaman (in command)

– Myra and Henry S. Harper, and their Pekinese dog Sun Yat Sen

– Charlotte Wardle Cardeza and her son Thomas

– Frederic and Margaretta Spedden with their son Robert

– Albert and Vera Dick

Lifeboat 4 (Port)

Launch time: Approximately 1:50 a.m.

Officer(s) in charge: Second Officer Charles Lightoller; Quartermaster Walter Perkis (placed in command)

Rated capacity: 65 persons

Estimated number aboard at launch: Approximately 34

Lifeboat 4 was the last of the wooden lifeboats to be lowered. To allow boarding, windows in the Promenade enclosure were forced open, and deck chairs were stacked to form makeshift steps. While men were generally excluded, one adolescent boy was permitted to enter after his father intervened. After launch, Perkis maneuvered the boat along the ship's side to search for additional passengers at open gangways but found none.

Shortly after Titanic sank, Lifeboat 4 immediately returned to the wreck site, making it the only lifeboat to do so without delay. It recovered several men from the water, though two later died from exposure.

Lifeboat 4 later received additional survivors transferred from Lifeboat 14 and Collapsible Boat D. By daylight, the boat was heavily occupied but remained seaworthy.

Lifeboat 4 reached RMS Carpathia at approximately 8:00.

Selected occupants:

– Madeleine Talmage Astor, with her maid and nurse

– Emily Borie Ryerson and her children

– Lucile Polk Carter and her children

Lifeboat 5 (Starboard)

Launch time: Approximately 12:55 a.m.

Officer(s) in charge: First Officer William Murdoch; Third Officer Herbert Pitman (placed in command)

Rated capacity: 65 persons

Estimated number aboard at launch: Approximately 36

Primarily launched with women and children, but at a time when many passengers remained unconvinced of the seriousness of the situation. Several declined to board. White Star Line chairman J. Bruce Ismay actively urged Pitman to begin loading women and children and assisted in directing passengers into the boat.

The lowering of Lifeboat 5 was slow and difficult. Newly painted pulleys and stiff ropes caused the boat to descend unevenly and in jerks. Following Titanic's sinking, several occupants were transferred to Lifeboat 7. Pitman proposed returning to the wreck site for rescue but abandoned the attempt after protests from passengers who feared the risk. The decision weighed on Pitman for the rest of his life.

RMS Carpathia rescued lifeboat 5 at approximately 6:00 a.m.

Selected occupants:

– Herbert Pitman, Third Officer

– Ruth Dodge and her son Washington Dodge Jr. (the first child placed in a lifeboat)

– Henry and Clara Frauenthal

– Karl Behr and members of the Beckwith family

Lifeboat 6 (Port)

Launch time: Approximately 12:55 a.m.

Officer(s) in charge: Captain Edward J. Smith; Second Officer Charles Lightoller; Quartermaster Robert Hichens (placed in command)

Rated capacity: 65 persons

Estimated number aboard at launch: Approximately 24

Lifeboat 6 was launched significantly under capacity. Margaret "Molly" Brown did not board voluntarily but was physically placed into the boat by a crewman as it was being lowered.

During lowering, concerns about insufficient manpower led Lightoller to request assistance from experienced personnel on deck. Major Arthur Godfrey Peuchen volunteered and descended into the boat, becoming the only adult male passenger permitted by Lightoller to board a lifeboat.

Relations aboard Lifeboat 6 were strained. Hichens and Peuchen clashed over authority and rowing duties. After Titanic sank, repeated appeals to return to rescue people in

the water were rejected by Hichens. He also resisted efforts
by female passengers to assist with rowing to keep warm.
Despite his objections, Margaret Brown organized the
women into rowing shifts, with support from other
passengers.

Lifeboat 6 later tied up with Lifeboat 16 and remained at
sea for several hours. One passenger, Mrs. Elizabeth
Rothschild, brought a Pomeranian aboard, one of the few
dogs to survive the disaster.

Lifeboat 6 rowing towards RMS Carpathia on April 15, 1912

Lifeboat 6 was among the last boats to reach RMS
Carpathia, coming alongside at approximately 8:00 a.m.

Selected occupants:

– Robert Hichens, Quartermaster (in command)

– Frederick Fleet, Lookout

– Margaret Brown

– Helen Churchill Candee

– Arthur Godfrey Peuchen

Lifeboat 7 (Starboard)

Launch time: Approximately 12:45 a.m.

Officer(s) in charge: First Officer William Murdoch; Fifth Officer Harold Lowe

Rated capacity: 65 persons

Estimated number aboard at launch: Approximately 28

Lifeboat 7 was the first lifeboat launched. Testimony given later indicated that officers were concerned about the structural integrity of the lifeboats if lowered fully loaded and intended to add people once they reached the water.

Lifeboat 7 was launched without its drain plug in place, causing water to enter the boat. The leak was temporarily controlled using clothing, but the occupants sat with their feet in freezing water. After Titanic sank at 2:20 a.m., those aboard heard the cries of people in the water. The occupants rejected a suggestion to return and render assistance.

The lifeboat drifted for some time before coming alongside Lifeboat 5. Several passengers were transferred from Lifeboat 5 into Lifeboat 7 due to overcrowding, after which the two boats were lashed together for the remainder of the night. Lifeboat 7 separated from Lifeboat 5 in daylight and was later recovered by RMS Carpathia.

Selected occupants:

– Dorothy Gibson, actress

– Margaret Hays

– Archie Jewell, lookout

– Alfred Nourney

Lifeboat 8 (Port)

Launch time: Approximately 1:10 a.m.

Officer(s) in charge: Captain Edward J. Smith; Chief Officer Henry Wilde; Able Seaman Thomas William Jones (placed in command)

Rated capacity: 65 persons

Estimated number aboard at launch: Approximately 27

Lifeboat 8 was the first lifeboat lowered on the port side. During loading, Isidor and Ida Straus were offered places, but both refused. They were last seen together on deck. Major Archibald Butt escorted a female passenger to the boat and assisted others before remaining aboard. Following the sinking, Jones proposed returning for rescue, but the majority objected, fearing the boat would be swamped. One passenger, Noëlle, Countess of Rothes, took an active role in managing the boat, assisting with steering, rowing, and organizing occupants. They spent several hours rowing toward lights believed to be another ship. At daylight, the boat reversed course when RMS Carpathia was sighted approaching from the opposite direction.

Lifeboat 8 was recovered at approximately 7:30 a.m.

Selected occupants:

– Noëlle, Countess of Rothes

– Marie Grice Young

– Ella Holmes White

Lifeboat 9 (Starboard)

Launch time: Approximately 1:20 a.m.

Officer(s) in charge: First Officer William Murdoch; Sixth Officer James Moody; Purser Hugh McElroy; Boatswain's Mate Albert Hames (placed in command)

Rated capacity: 65 persons

Estimated number aboard at launch: Approximately 40

Lifeboat 9 was launched with primarily women, and a small number of men were admitted only after no other women came forward. Several passengers initially resisted boarding. One elderly woman refused outright and returned below decks. May Futrelle was also reluctant to leave until urged strongly by her husband, novelist Jacques Futrelle, who remained behind and later perished. Benjamin Guggenheim escorted his companion and her maid into Lifeboat 9 before retiring to his stateroom. Other male passengers were prevented from boarding despite appeals from women already in the boat.

Lifeboat 9 remained clear of the wreck site and did not attempt a return, and was recovered at approximately 6:15.

Selected occupants:

– May Futrelle

– Léontine Aubart

– Kate Buss

Lifeboat 10 (Port)

Launch time: Approximately 1:47 a.m.

Officer(s) in charge: Chief Officer Henry Wilde; First Officer William Murdoch; Able Seaman Edward Buley (placed in command)

Rated capacity: 65 persons

Estimated number aboard at launch: Approximately 57

Lifeboat 10 was launched when Titanic was listing heavily to port, creating a widening gap between the deck and the lifeboats and making boarding increasingly hazardous. As urgency increased, loading became rapid and chaotic. Several passengers boarded with difficulty, including one woman who narrowly avoided falling between the ship and the boat. Children were rushed aboard, and at least one infant was passed directly into the lifeboat. A third-class passenger jumped into the boat as it was being lowered.

Lifeboat 10 was the second-to-last lifeboat recovered by RMS Carpathia, coming alongside at approximately 8:00 a.m.

Selected occupants:

– Edward Buley, Able Seaman (in command)

– Millvina Dean, with her mother and brother

– Masabumi Hosono

– Barbara West and her family

Lifeboat 11 (Starboard)

Launch time: Approximately 1:37 a.m.

Officer(s) in charge: First Officer William Murdoch; Able Seaman Sidney Humphreys (placed in command)

Rated capacity: 65 persons

Estimated number aboard at launch: Approximately 70

Lifeboat 11 departed heavily loaded, carrying an estimated 70 persons aboard, exceeding its rated capacity. During loading, one steward was knocked into the boat while assisting passengers, reflecting the increasingly crowded and urgent conditions on deck. A Second Class mother was initially prevented from boarding after her children were placed aboard, but ultimately succeeded in entering. However, one of her daughters was left behind and directed to another lifeboat. Upon reaching the water, Lifeboat 11 was nearly swamped by a powerful stream of water being discharged from the ship in an attempt to control flooding. Passengers were tightly packed, and some were forced to stand as the boat pulled away.

Lifeboat 11 was recovered by RMS Carpathia at approximately 7:00 a.m.

Selected occupants:

– Sidney Humphreys, Able Seaman (in command)

– Edith Louise Rosenbaum

– Alice Catherine Cooper

– Annie Robinson, stewardess

– Jane Quick and her daughters May and Winnifred

Lifeboat 12 (Port)

Launch time: Approximately 1:35 a.m.

Officer(s) in charge: Chief Officer Henry Wilde; Second Officer Charles Lightoller; Able Seaman John Poingdestre (placed in command)

Rated capacity: 65 persons

Estimated number aboard at launch: Approximately 28–30

Lifeboat 12 was lowered with primarily second-class passengers and crew.

After Titanic sank, Lifeboat 12 became heavily involved in redistribution and rescue operations, coordinating with Lifeboats 4, 10, 14, and Collapsible D. Later, Lifeboat 12—together with Lifeboat 4—responded to Second Officer Lightoller's whistle from the overturned Collapsible B. The boat rescued approximately 16 survivors standing on the upturned hull. Command of Lifeboat 12 subsequently passed to Lightoller.

By the end of these transfers and rescue efforts, Lifeboat 12 was heavily overloaded, carrying an estimated 60 to 70 persons, well beyond its intended capacity. Despite this, the boat remained afloat and operational.

Lifeboat 12 was the last lifeboat recovered by RMS Carpathia, coming alongside at approximately 8:30 a.m.

Selected occupants:

– John Poingdestre, Able Seaman (initially in command)

– Charles Lightoller, Second Officer (later in command)

– Frederick Clench, Able Seaman

Lifeboat 13 (Starboard)

Launch time: Approximately 1:43 a.m.

Officer(s) in charge: First Officer William Murdoch; Sixth Officer James Moody; Leading Fireman Frederick William Barrett (placed in command)

Rated capacity: 65 persons

Estimated number aboard at launch: Approximately 70

Lifeboat 13 was launched heavily occupied, carrying an estimated 70 persons aboard. The majority of passengers were women and children from Second and Third Class.

While being lowered, Lifeboat 13 was nearly swamped by a powerful stream of water being expelled from the ship's condenser exhaust. Occupants were forced to fend the boat off using oars and spars. The wash from the exhaust caused the boat to drift directly beneath Lifeboat 15, which was descending at the same time. Lifeboat 15's lowering was halted just in time to avoid crushing Lifeboat 13. The falls of Lifeboat 13 jammed and had to be cut free before the boat could clear the ship. Lifeboat 13 was recovered by RMS Carpathia at approximately 6:30 a.m.

Selected occupants:

– Frederick William Barrett, Leading Fireman (in command)

– Lawrence Beesley

– Reginald Robinson Lee, Lookout

– Frederick Dent Ray

Lifeboat 14 (Port)

Launch time: Approximately 1:30 a.m.

Officer(s) in charge: Chief Officer Henry Wilde; Second Officer Charles Lightoller; Fifth Officer Harold Godfrey Lowe; Sixth Officer James Moody; Harold Godfrey Lowe (placed in command)

Rated capacity: 65 persons

Estimated number aboard at launch: Approximately 40

Lifeboat 14 launched as Titanic was already listing noticeably. After Titanic sank, Lowe gathered several nearby boats—Lifeboats 4, 10, 12, and Collapsible D—and redistributed passengers to reduce overcrowding. He then assembled a volunteer crew and returned Lifeboat 14 to the wreck site in an attempt to rescue survivors from the water.

Lifeboat 14 was one of only two boats to return for rescue. Four men were pulled from the sea; one later died, while three survived. Several hours later, the survivors from Collapsible Boat A, which was near sinking, were brought aboard Lifeboat 14. Lowe also rigged a mast and sail to improve speed and maneuverability, making

Lifeboat 14 the only lifeboat to employ sail power during the rescue efforts.

Lifeboat 14 reached RMS Carpathia at approximately 7:15.

Selected occupants:

– Eva Hart and her mother Esther Hart

– Edith Eileen Brown and her mother Elizabeth

– Marjorie Collyer and her mother Charlotte

Lifeboat 15 (Starboard)

Launch time: Approximately 1:45 a.m.

Officer(s) in charge: First Officer William Murdoch; Sixth Officer James Moody; Fireman Frank Dymond (placed in command)

Rated capacity: 65 persons

Estimated number aboard at launch: Approximately 70

Lifeboat 15 was lowered almost simultaneously with Lifeboat 13, and departed heavily loaded, with an estimated 70 persons aboard, making it one of the most crowded boats launched from Titanic.

The boat sat extremely low in the water at launch, with later testimony describing the gunwales as nearly awash.

Due to the heavy load, conditions aboard were cramped and precarious. Passengers reported that even slight movement caused the boat to dip close to the waterline. Despite this, Lifeboat 15 cleared the ship safely and remained afloat throughout the night.

Lifeboat 15 was among the last boats recovered by RMS Carpathia, coming alongside at approximately 7:30 a.m.

Selected occupants:

– Frank Dymond, Fireman (in command)

– Lillian Asplund, with her mother Selma and brother Felix

– Arthur John Priest, Fireman

– Alfred Frank Evans, Lookout

– George Cavell, Trimmer

Lifeboat 16 (Port)

Launch time: Approximately 1:25 a.m.

Officer(s) in charge: Chief Officer Henry Wilde; Sixth Officer James Moody; Master-at-Arms Joseph Henry Bailey (placed in command)

Rated capacity: 65 persons

Estimated number aboard at launch: Approximately 53

Lifeboat 16 was launched with a comparatively large number of passengers, most of whom were women and children from Second and Third Class. At one point, it encountered Lifeboat 6 and transferred a fireman to assist with rowing.

Accounts from Third Class passengers describe the embarkation as orderly and calm, with little sense of panic. The ship remained fully illuminated, and music continued to play as the lifeboats were launched. Passengers later recalled witnessing Titanic's final breakup and the cries from the water that followed, followed by an abrupt silence. Survivors later described profound shock and emotional distress following rescue, with many passengers struggling to process what they had witnessed during the night.

Selected occupants:

– – Violet Constance Jessop, stewardess

– Evelyn Marsden, stewardess

– Elizabeth Leather, stewardess

– Margaret Mannion

Collapsible Lifeboat A (Starboard)

Launch time: Not successfully launched; washed off the deck during the final plunge.

Officer(s) in charge: Chief Officer Henry Wilde; First Officer William Murdoch; Sixth Officer James Moody

Rated capacity: 47 persons

Estimated number aboard: Unknown at separation; approximately 14 survivors remained alive

Collapsible Lifeboat A was brought onto the Boat Deck upright at approximately 2:05 a.m. and was in the process of being launched when Titanic's final plunge caused the lifeboat to be washed off the deck at approximately 2:15 a.m. In the ensuing chaos, the boat drifted away from the ship, partially submerged, with water flooding the interior. Several passengers entered the boat directly from the sea.

Many occupants succumbed to hypothermia or fell back into the water during the night. By morning, only about 14 people remained alive aboard Collapsible A.

Survivors from Collapsible Lifeboat A were rescued by Lifeboat 14 during a return to the wreck site. Some survivors were later transferred to Collapsible Lifeboat D. Survivors were taken aboard RMS Carpathia via other lifeboats. Collapsible Lifeboat A itself was later recovered approximately one month after the disaster with several bodies still aboard.

Selected occupants:

– Rhoda Mary Abbott

– Olaus Abelseth

Collapsible Lifeboat B (Port)

Launch time: Not launched; washed off the deck during the final plunge.

Officer(s) in charge: Second Officer Charles Lightoller (assumed command after capsizing)

Rated capacity: 47 persons

Estimated number aboard: Approximately 30–35 initially on hull; about 28 survived until transfer

At approximately 2:10 a.m., Second Officer Lightoller attempted to free the boat from the roof of the officers' quarters. During the attempt, the lifeboat broke through the ramp and landed upside down on the Boat Deck. There was no opportunity to right it before Titanic entered its final plunge.

At approximately 2:15 a.m., water swept across the Boat Deck, washing the overturned lifeboat and numerous people into the sea.

As the ship sank, the forward funnel collapsed into the water, forcing Collapsible B farther from the wreck. Several dozen men managed to climb onto the overturned hull, including Lightoller, as well as senior crew members and first-class passengers. Wireless operator Harold Bride escaped from beneath the hull after being temporarily trapped in an air pocket.

The boat floated keel-up, supported by a diminishing air pocket beneath it. As the night progressed, the hull settled lower in the water and became increasingly unstable.

Those clinging to the hull endured exposure to freezing water. Lightoller organized the men into two balanced lines along the hull to counteract rolling caused by the swell. Despite these efforts, exhaustion and hypothermia caused several men to slip into the water and die during the night.

By morning, approximately 28 survivors remained alive. They were transferred to other lifeboats before the final rescue. Survivors from Collapsible B were later taken aboard RMS Carpathia via other lifeboats. The overturned hull itself was later sighted adrift by recovery vessels in the days following the disaster.

Selected occupants:

– – Harold Bride, Wireless Operator

– Archibald Gracie IV

– Charles John Joughin, Chief Baker

– Jack Thayer

Collapsible Boat B, found adrift by the ship Mackay-Bennett during its mission to recover the bodies of those who died in the disaster.

Collapsible Lifeboat C (Starboard)

Launch time: Approximately 2:00 a.m.

Officer(s) in charge: Chief Officer Henry Wilde; First Officer William Murdoch; Quartermaster George Rowe (placed in command)

Rated capacity: 47 persons

Estimated number aboard at launch: Approximately 43

Collapsible Lifeboat C was the first of the collapsible lifeboats to be launched. By this point, most forward lifeboats had already departed, and the remaining crowd on deck had shifted aft as the bow settled lower in the water.

During loading, a group of stewards and third-class passengers attempted to rush the boat but were driven back after warning shots were fired. After repeated calls for women and children, the remaining spaces were filled by men. Among those who boarded was White Star Line chairman J. Bruce Ismay, whose survival later became a significant source of public controversy. As the boat descended, Titanic's growing list caused it to strike the hull, and occupants were forced to fend it off using hands and oars.

Collapsible Lifeboat C was recovered by RMS Carpathia, arriving at approximately 5:45 a.m.

Selected occupants:

– J. Bruce Ismay

– Frank Goldsmith and his mother Emily

– William E. Carter

Collapsible Lifeboat D (Port)

Launch time: Approximately 2:05 a.m.

Officer(s) in charge: Chief Officer Henry Wilde; Second Officer Charles Lightoller; Quartermaster Arthur Bright (placed in command)

Rated capacity: 47 persons

Estimated number aboard at launch: Approximately 20

Collapsible Lifeboat D was the last lifeboat launched from the ship; all other boats were washed off the deck as it sank. Crew members strictly enforced the "women and children first" policy resulting in it leaving significantly under capacity. Two young boys, later known as the "Titanic Orphans," were brought by a passenger who did not board and perished in the sinking. Another young child, previously separated from his family, was also placed in the lifeboat by crew members. Several male passengers later entered the boat by jumping from A Deck. Following the sinking, Collapsible D received additional survivors transferred from Collapsible Boat A, increasing the number of occupants substantially. Collapsible Lifeboat D reached RMS Carpathia at approximately 7:15 a.m.

Selected occupants:

– Michel Marcel Navratil and his brother Edmond

– Mauritz Håkan Björnström-Steffansson

– Irene Wallach Harris

Chart of Survivors

Passengers	Category	Number on board	Percentage by total on board	Number saved	Number lost	Percentage saved	Percentage lost	Percentage saved by total on board	Percentage lost by total on board
Children	First Class	6	0.3%	5	1	83%	17%	0.2%	< 0.1%
	Second Class	24	1.1%	24	0	100%	0%	1.1%	0%
	Third Class	79	3.6%	27	52	34%	66%	1.2%	2.4%
	Total	109	5%	56	53	51%	49%	2.5%	2.4%
Women	First Class	144	6.5%	140	4	97%	3%	6.3%	0.2%
	Second Class	93	4.2%	80	13	86%	14%	3.6%	0.6%
	Third Class	165	7.4%	76	89	46%	54%	3.4%	4.0%
	Crew	23	1.0%	20	3	87%	13%	0.9%	0.1%
	Total	425	19.1%	316	109	74%	26%	14.2%	4.9%
Men	First Class	175	7.9%	57	118	33%	67%	2.6%	5.3%
	Second Class	168	7.6%	14	154	8%	92%	0.6%	6.9%
	Third Class	462	20.8%	75	387	16%	84%	3.3%	17.4%
	Crew	885	39.8%	192	693	22%	78%	8.6%	31.2%
	Total	1,690	75.9%	338	1,352	20%	80%	15.2%	60.8%
Total	All	2,224	100%	710	1,514	32%	68%	31.9%	68.1%

Pregnant Women of Titanic

By mid-January 1913, nine babies had been born to mothers who had survived the Titanic. At least two pregnant women also perished in the sinking.

First Class

Madeleine Astor was 18 years old, traveling with her husband, John Jacob Astor, and was five months pregnant during the voyage. John did not survive the sinking. Their son, John Jacob, was born four months after the disaster, on 14th August 1912. John Jacob had a son and a daughter and lived until 26th June 1992.

Mary Graham Carmichael Marvin was 18 years old, traveling home to New York from her honeymoon with her husband, Daniel Warner Marvin. She was rescued in Lifeboat 10, but her husband did not survive. She gave birth to a daughter, Mary Margaret Elizabeth Marvin, on October 21, 1912. Mary Margaret Elizabeth Marvin lived until October 7, 1993.

Mary Eloise Hughes Smith was 18 years old, traveling home to America from her honeymoon with her husband, Lucian Philip Smith. Mary Smith was rescued in Lifeboat 6; her husband was not saved. She gave birth to Lucian Philip Smith on November 29, 1912; He lived until October 1971.

Second Class

Mary Emma Corey, aged 32, was returning to America from Burma because of her pregnancy. She was lost in the disaster.

Argene Del Carlo was traveling from Italy to America with her husband, Sebastiano Del Carlo, and was roughly 8 weeks pregnant at the time of the sinking. Her husband did not survive. She gave birth to a baby girl, Maria Salvata Del Carlo, on November 14, 1912, in Italy.

Juliette Marie Louise Laroche was 22 years old, traveling from France to her husband's native Haiti. She was accompanied by her husband, Joseph Philippe Lemercier Laroche, their 3-year-old daughter, Simonne, and their 1-year-old daughter, Louise. She was also roughly 8 weeks pregnant with her third child. Juliette Laroche and her daughters were rescued. Her husband was lost. She travelled back to France after the disaster, and gave birth to a son, Joseph LaRoche, Jr, on 17th December 1912. Joseph LaRoche, Jr, married, had children, and lived until 17th January 1987.

Adal Na Allah was a second-class passenger making her way from Lebanon to her home in America. Roughly 17 years old and nearly 8 weeks pregnant, she survived the sinking, but her husband was lost. She gave birth to a son on 9th December 1912, but he died shortly after he was born.

Ada Mary West was 33 years old and emigrating from Britain to America with her husband, Edwy Arthur West, and their daughters, 4-year-old Constance Miriam and 10-month-old Barbara Joyce. She was also four months pregnant with their third child. Ada West and her daughters were rescued, but her husband was not. She gave birth to a daughter, Edwyna Joan West, on 14th September 1912. Edwyna lived until 1969.

Third Class

Maria Mathilda Backström was a 33-year-old passenger traveling from Finland to America with her husband. She was seven months pregnant and survived by boarding the last lifeboat to be successfully lowered from the ship. Her husband and brothers were lost. She gave birth to Alfhild Maria in June 1912 in Finland.

Hannah O'Brien was 27 years old and emigrating from Ireland to America with her husband, Thomas O'Brien. She was four months pregnant. Her husband did not survive. Hannah O'Brien gave birth to a daughter, Marion Columba O'Brien, on September 3, 1912. Marion O'Brien lived until July 4, 1994.

A Canine Eulogy

The ship's log says that twelve dogs boarded Titanic:

- Two Airedales
- King Charles Spaniel
- Fox Terrier
- Chow Chow
- Poodle
- French Bulldog
- Great Dane
- Newfoundland.
- Two Pomeranians
- Pekingese

One woman lived the rest of her life haunted by the memory of her Poodle clinging to her pajamas as she left her cabin and her dog behind.

Another passenger, Ann Elizabeth Isham, boarded the Titanic in Cherbourg with her Great Dane. She refused to leave the ship without her dog, which was too large to fit in a lifeboat. Ann Isham was one of four first-class female passengers who died on the Titanic. There are accounts, though unsubstantiated, that her body, with her arms wrapped around the dog, was later found by a recovery ship.

Margaret Bechstein Hays's Pomeranian (Lifeboat 7)

Margaret Hays, a first-class passenger, wrapped her Pomeranian in blankets and took it with her into Lifeboat 7, the first boat launched.

The three surviving dogs of Titanic

John Jacob Astor and his Airedale, Kitty, and Gamin de Pycombe
with his champion French Bulldog.

The Harpers' Pekingese "Sun Yat Sen" (Lifeboat 3)

Henry and Myra Harper, also first-class passengers, took
their Pekingese, "Sun Yat Sen," into Lifeboat 3. As to the
rationale for how a pet made it into a boat while so many

240

people did not, Henry S. Harper, a publishing magnate, replied: "There seemed to be lots of room, and nobody made any objection."

The Rothchilds' Pomeranian (Lifeboat 6)
First-class passenger Elizabeth Jane Rothschild hid the dog until the following morning, when the RMS Carpathia rescued those on Lifeboat 6. The crew had initially refused to take the dog on board, but Elizabeth insisted. Mr. Rothschild didn't survive the sinking.

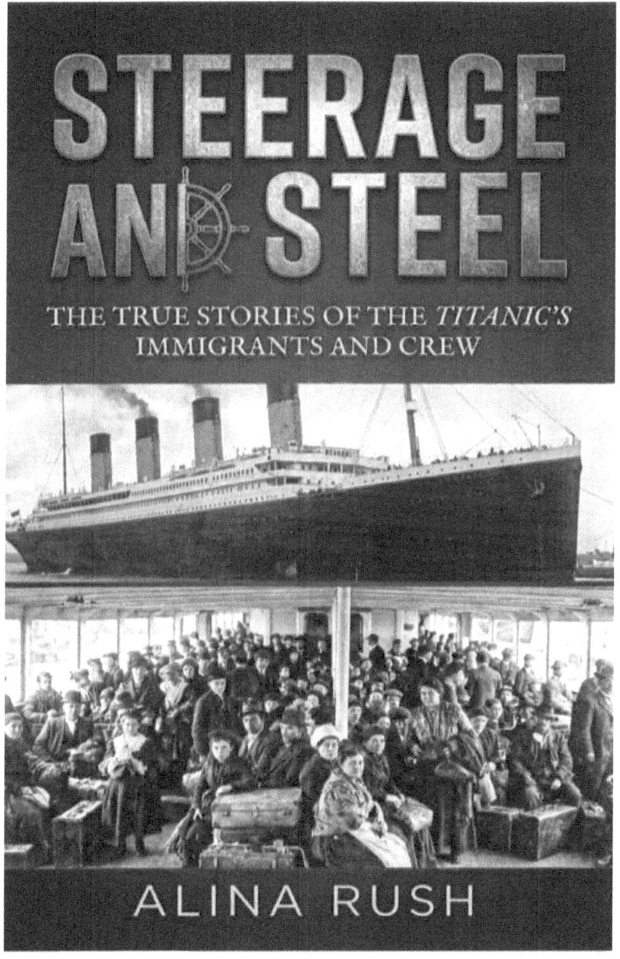
STEERAGE
AND STEEL
THE TRUE STORIES OF THE *TITANIC'S*
IMMIGRANTS AND CREW
ALINA RUSH

Introduction

The first thing most people remember about Titanic is what happened on the top decks: the band, the lifeboats, the grand staircase, the famous names. That version of the story is not wrong—but it is incomplete in the way that myths are incomplete. It is the Titanic remembered from above.

This book begins below.

Steerage was not just "third class"—it was an ecosystem of families, single travelers, and communities in motion. Down below, families lay shoulder to shoulder in narrow bunks, surrounded by trunks, bundled bedding, and the weight of everything they could not afford to bring. Languages overlapped in the corridors—Irish, Swedish, Finnish, Italian, Arabic, English—each voice carrying the same hope in different words: a new start.

The crew was not a single category either; it was a hierarchy of labor, authority, and exhaustion. In the workspaces beyond the passenger decks, men shoveled coal for furnace heat, hauled ash, oiled machinery, and measured their shifts not by sunlight but by whistles and schedules. Wireless operators, stewards, and lookouts kept the ship functioning with their invisible labor. The ship's luxury depended on them. Its speed depended on their bodies. Its order depended on their obedience.

They are rarely the center of Titanic's story. They should be.

Titanic was not only a maritime disaster. It was a floating map of the early twentieth century—of wealth and poverty, of empire and industry, of migration and ambition, of rules designed to separate people and keep them in their place. Class was built into the ship's architecture. It shaped where you slept, what you ate, which corridors you could walk through, which doors you could open, which information reached you first, and what chances you had when everything went wrong.

That is why the lower decks matter. Not because they provide a grittier backdrop for the same famous tale, but because they reveal Titanic as it truly was: a society under steam.

This book follows two groups whose experiences are often treated as footnotes—immigrants and crew—not because their stories are marginal, but because they are central to what Titanic meant. The immigrants carried the future in battered luggage: the promise of jobs, family reunions, escape from hardship, and a chance at dignity on the far side of the Atlantic. The crew carried the ship itself: stokers and trimmers feeding the boilers, greasers keeping engines alive, stewards running corridors, sailors tending lines, and workers whose names never became legend because their work was always unseen.

Their worlds overlapped more than the usual retellings admit. Both groups lived inside the unseen machinery of modern life: schedules, compartments, rules, gatekeeping, and the belief—explicit and enforced—that some lives were meant to have more access than others.
When the collision came, those differences did not vanish. They sharpened.

Most narratives of the sinking focus on the ship's command and its officers' decisions. Titanic was not commanded into tragedy by a single decision or failure. It was built to carry inequality across an ocean, and when crisis struck, inequality became destiny for many.

This book stays close to the record: passenger lists, crew rosters, contemporary newspaper reporting, official investigations, letters, memoirs, and the scattered fragments families saved because they could not bear to lose everything. Where the record is uncertain, it will be treated as uncertain. Where testimony conflicts, the conflict will be shown. If a detail survives only as legend, it will be labeled as such, not smuggled in as fact.

But this is not a story made only of documents. It is a story made of people.

It is a mother counting children in a chaotic corridor with instructions she cannot fully understand. It is a father calculating, in a few seconds, whether to stay with his family or race upward to find help. It is a young man traveling alone or a crewman who knows the ship by heart and still cannot control what water will do once it has found a way in.

It is the quiet, brutal truth that "women and children first" meant something different depending on which deck you lived on and which doors were between you and the boats.

It is also the aftermath—because for immigrants and crew, the story does not end when the Carpathia arrives. Survival was not a clean ending. It meant poverty, injuries, grief, and the strange burden of being alive when others were not. For families who lost everyone, the aftermath was paperwork and silence: bodies unidentified, stories flattened into a line on a list. For the crew, it was often blame without recognition—asked to answer for a catastrophe that the world insisted must have been someone's fault.

And yet, amid all that, there is what makes these histories worth telling: resilience. The stubborn insistence that the class of ticket does not measure a life it carried. The truth is that some of the most consequential stories in history belong to people who never had a platform, never wrote a memoir, and never saw their names on a plaque.

If you came to this book looking for the Titanic you already know—the famous passengers, the grand symbols—you will still find the ship's outlines here, because that Titanic is the setting no one can ignore. But the center of gravity shifts. The emphasis turns to the spaces most retellings rush past: the narrow stairwells, gates, and corridors, and the boiler rooms, and the deck edges where instruction turned into panic and panic turned into fate.

This is Titanic as experienced by the people who made it move, and the people who trusted it with everything they owned.

This is the story carried in steerage and forged in steel.

"Pride goeth before destruction, and a haughty spirit before a fall."

—Book of Proverbs, 16:18

TITANIC DID NOT SIMPLY carry people across the Atlantic. It arranged them.

Before a single lifeboat was swung out, before a single iceberg warning was logged, the ship had already made its most consequential decision: it turned social class into architecture. The divisions that shaped daily life on land — money, language, status, labor — were built into the steel corridors, deck access, dining rooms, and doors.

Titanic, Public Domain

If you traveled first class, the ship was a statement. If you traveled in steerage, it was a system. If you worked the voyage, it was a machine you fed with hours, sweat, and compliance.

The Two Titanics

There were, in practice, at least two Titanics moving through the same water.

The public Titanic was the one photographed, described, and sold to the world. A ship of gleaming public rooms, wide promenades, and polished ritual. It was built to reassure. The White Star Line's promise was not only speed; it was stability. The ship was marketed as modern, safe, and comfortable, a floating hotel that made the Atlantic feel smaller and less frightening.
But the hidden Titanic was the one that made the public Titanic possible. It was a ship of narrow passageways, shared spaces, strict rules, and controlled movement. It was a ship where work and migration were not themes but realities. The people there did not talk about the ship as a marvel. They talked about what it cost, what it meant, and what it might change.

For many immigrant families, Titanic was a single pivot point: the moment between a life they were leaving and one they hoped would be better. They carried addresses on paper, names of relatives to find, the promise of jobs, and the belief that America could be remade through endurance.

For crew members, Titanic represented something different: a contract, a wage, a hierarchy. For the crew, the Atlantic was not an ocean to cross; it was a workplace to endure.

These realities existed on the same ship, yet they did not receive the same protections, information, or opportunities. That is not moral commentary. It is a structural description. And structure matters.

What "Steerage" Really Meant

"Third class" sounds tidy. "Steerage" sounds like something older, rougher, and less dignified—and the language matters because it reveals what was expected.

Steerage passengers came from different nations, religions, trades, family structures, and social worlds. Some were traveling alone, aiming to earn money and send it home. Others were families in motion, heading toward relatives already settled. Some were skilled workers. Some were agricultural laborers. Some were fleeing political pressures, religious constraints, or local economies that had failed them.

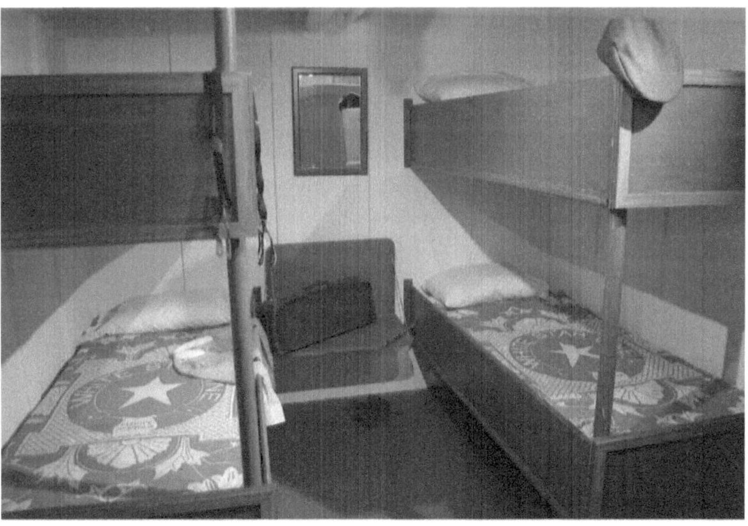

Titanic The Artifact Exhibition Boston Third Class Cabin 2025

What they shared was not identity. It was placement.

Steerage accommodations were designed for volume, sanitation, and control, not for comfort or leisure. Most passengers slept in shared cabins or dormitory-style spaces, often with stacked berths. Privacy was minimal. Noise and smells carried. The ship was engineered to reduce disease risk compared with older steerage travel, but it was still a crowded living environment.

Third-class passengers had access to a male-only smoking room, two dining rooms (divided by a bulkhead), and a general room that served as both a lounge and a nursery, which became a recreational area each evening.

Cabins in third class included bunk beds for 4 to 6 people, a sink, and a small wardrobe. Private toilets in the ship's cabins were unheard of and not even available in second class. Large, well-maintained public toilets, similar to those we see today in public spaces and restaurants, were provided, along with showers and baths.

The third-class experience also depended on who one traveled with. Entire clusters of passengers from the same region or language group were sometimes found aboard, forming temporary communities—translating rules, sharing information, and helping one another navigate shipboard life.

It is essential to say this plainly: steerage life was not uniformly miserable. Many immigrants were accustomed to hardship and saw the ship's conditions as a tolerable price for a new start. But steerage life was always constrained, and constraints become critical in an emergency.

Because when the ship struck the iceberg, steerage passengers did not begin the night with equal access to the outside decks. They began it with questions: What happened? Where do we go? Which corridor leads upward? Which door is for us? Who will translate? Will we be permitted through?

A ship built to manage people smoothly in ordinary times can become a trap when time becomes extraordinary.

The Crew: Not One Group, But a Ladder of Labor

Titanic's crew is often spoken of as if it were a single class of men in uniform. However, on a large passenger liner, crew work was divided into departments with distinct authorities, risks, and levels of visibility. Passengers constantly saw some crew members: stewards, dining-room staff, officers, and perhaps a few deckhands. Others worked out of sight: engine-room teams, firemen, trimmers, greasers—men whose labor powered the ship but rarely entered the public imagination.

There was a ladder within the labor force itself. Officers held authority and status. Many other crew members were disposable, as industrial labor often is: replaceable bodies assigned to exhausting work.

Some crew roles were physically punishing even in regular operation. Boiler-room and engine-room work involved heat, coal dust, noise, and constant motion. It was not heroic in the romantic sense. It was relentless. It was measured in shifts and endurance.

This matters for the same reason as steerage issues of structure: in a disaster, you do not suddenly become equal.

You move according to the job you were hired to do and the space you were assigned to inhabit.

A crewman assigned below decks could not simply abandon his post without consequences—formal, cultural, and practical. In a crisis, some men stayed because they were ordered to. Some stayed because they believed it was the right thing. Some stayed because leaving would have been physically difficult or impossible. The result is the same: the ship's "hidden" workforce often had less opportunity to reach safety than the people they served.

The Gatekeeping Ship

Ships of this era were designed with controlled access: class-segregated stairways, corridors that funneled people toward specific spaces, and doors that directed traffic. Some of these boundaries were cultural—unspoken rules reinforced by staff. Others were literal—gates, partitions, posted areas, and staffed doors.

In ordinary times, such systems reduce chaos. They keep meals running. They prevent crowding. They preserve the illusion that different social worlds can coexist without friction.

In crisis, those same systems can delay information, slow evacuation, and turn uncertainty into panic. For immigrants unfamiliar with the ship's layout—especially those navigating language barriers—delay is not a minor inconvenience. Delay is survival math.

This is one of the core truths of Titanic: class shaped time. Time to learn what happened. Time to understand the orders. Time to reach the deck and find a boat. The time to decide.

When people argue about whether steerage was "held back," the debate often devolves into a simplistic accusation. The reality is that systems designed for control in normal operation perform poorly under stress. People within those systems make choices—some generous, some indifferent, some fearful, some cruel. The architecture itself quietly takes sides.

To tell the story correctly, we have to understand the ship before the collision: not as a legend, but as a functioning society. A ship that offered luxury to some, passage to others, and employment to many—then demanded that all of them respond to catastrophe from very different starting positions.

You can continue reading Steerage and Steel by finding it at www.unboundpressbooks.com, Amazon, Barnes & Noble or your local retailer.